Better Homes and Gardens®

After Work
Cook Book

© 1974 by Meredith Corporation, Des Moines, Iowa.
All Rights Reserved. Printed in the United States of America.
First Edition. Sixteenth Printing, 1982.
Library of Congress Catalog Card Number: 73-78909
ISBN: 0-696-00690-1

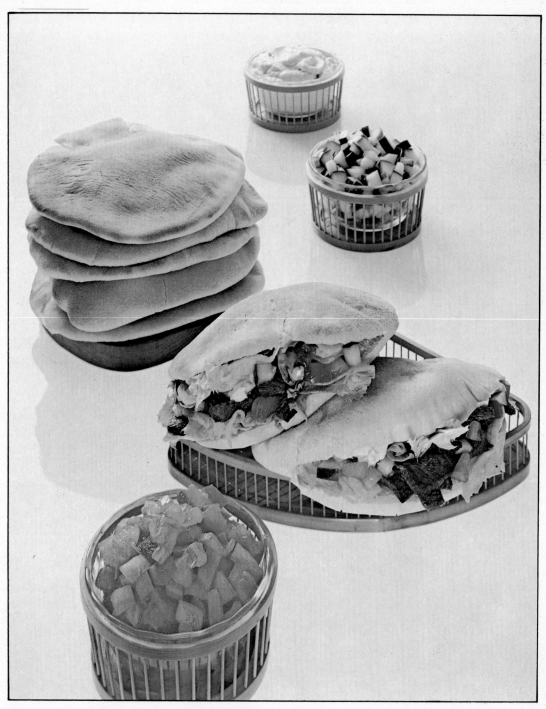

On the cover: *After work meals become exciting when you include these dishes. Clockwise from top* — Salad Burgers, Chicken-Rice Bake, Cottage Cheese-Cucumber Salad, Cheese-Stuffed Manicotti, *or Strawberry-Cheese Topping. (See index for pages.)*

Above: *Let everyone assemble at the table their own Greek-Style Sandwich. Fill the hollow* Bread Envelopes *with a marinated wine-beef filling, chopped lettuce, diced tomato, diced cucumber, and sour cream dip. (See recipes, pages 21 and 22.)*

Contents

BETTER HOMES AND GARDENS® BOOKS

Editorial Director: Don Dooley
Managing Editor: Malcolm E. Robinson   Art Director: John Berg
Asst. Managing Editor: Lawrence D. Clayton   Asst. Art Director: Randall Yontz
Food Editor: Nancy Morton
Senior Food Editor: Joyce Trollope
Associate Editors: Sharyl Heiken, Rosemary Corsiglia
Assistant Editors: Elizabeth Strait, Sandra Mapes
Designers: Harijs Priekulis, Tonya Rodriguez

Our seal assures you that every recipe in *After Work Cook Book* is endorsed by the Better Homes and Gardens Test Kitchen. Each recipe is tested for family appeal, practicality, and deliciousness.

To Busy Cooks Everywhere

If you're busy and you have to hurry home to cook meals for yourself, your family, or friends, *Better Homes and Gardens After Work Cook Book* is aimed squarely at you. And who isn't busy these days! Bachelors, college students, working mothers, and women employed outside the home surely are.

To help you make the best use of your limited meal preparation time, *After Work Cook Book* has been divided into three recipe sections, each based on the amount of time you can spend in the kitchen, plus a Special Helps section near the end of the book. This includes a list of basic kitchen equipment and supplies, advice on meal planning, food storage, and nutrition, plus menus using recipes from this book.

The first of the recipe sections, Cook Ahead, will be helpful when you know ahead of time that your schedule will be hectic. Here, you'll find recipes that can be made on weekends or the evening before, then put in the freezer or refrigerator until shortly before mealtime. When you are caught completely off-guard and need to prepare something in a hurry, make your selection from the In A Jiffy section. These recipes are ready to eat in 30 minutes or less. But no one is busy every night. So when you have a leisurely evening, prepare one of the recipes from the Make It Easy section. These recipes are simple to prepare and require little watching, allowing you time to relax.

Other notable features of the book include tip boxes, symbols accompanying recipes especially suitable for entertaining, and several recipes for two.

Remember, busy schedules and home-cooked meals can be coordinated. Just use the variety of recipes and helps in the *After Work Cook Book* and make the most of your limited time.

Serve tasty Barbecue-Sauced Kabobs *on a bed of parslied rice. Broil the beef, potato, and zucchini kabobs in a countertop broiler or under a regular broiler. Either way, this delicious main dish for four is ready in a jiffy. Pass the remaining zippy catsup sauce with the kabobs. (See recipe, page 37.)*

Cook Ahead

Does fitting food preparation into your after work hours mean skimpy meals night after night? If so, you'll welcome the variety of make-ahead main dishes, side dishes, and desserts in this section. Just prepare the food in your spare time on weekends or the evening before the meal, then store it in the freezer or refrigerator. When you arrive home from work, simply add the finishing touches and put the dish on to cook.

Do you like to entertain but can never find the time? Cook ahead and you won't need to get home much before the guests arrive. Plan your company menus around the recipes marked with the special entertaining symbol.

Also watch for the tip boxes scattered throughout this section. Use these ideas and hints to make meal preparation easier.

Enhance the platter of Dill-Sauced Salmon with fresh dill and lemon and lime slices. Add this make-ahead dish to your next entertaining menu. (See recipe, page 8.)

Main Dishes

Dill-Sauced Salmon

Elegant chilled salmon shown on pages 6 and 7—

4 fresh or frozen salmon steaks
  Boiling water
1 small onion, quartered
1 cup dairy sour cream
2 tablespoons finely
  chopped onion
2 teaspoons lemon juice
1 teaspoon dried dillweed

(ENTERTAINING SPECIAL)

Advance preparation: Thaw frozen fish. Place on greased rack in 10-inch skillet. Add boiling water to cover. Add quartered onion and 2 teaspoons salt. Simmer, covered, till fish flakes easily, 5 to 10 minutes. Carefully remove fish. Cover; chill well. Combine remaining ingredients; chill well.
Before serving: Spoon sour cream mixture over chilled salmon. Garnish with lemon and lime slices and fresh dillweed, if desired. Makes 4 servings.

Cauliflower-Tuna Ahoy

Advance preparation: Cook two 10-ounce packages frozen cauliflower according to package directions; drain and coarsely chop. Set aside. In large covered saucepan cook 1 cup fresh or frozen chopped onion in 2 tablespoons water. Stir in two 11-ounce cans condensed Cheddar cheese soup; one 6-ounce can sliced mushrooms, drained; ½ cup milk; 2 tablespoons snipped parsley; 1 teaspoon Worcestershire sauce; dash cayenne; and dash pepper. Drain two 6½- or 7-ounce cans tuna; break into chunks. Fold tuna and cauliflower into soup mixture. Spoon into two 1½-quart casseroles. Cover tightly. Seal; label; freeze up to 2 months.
Before serving: Bake frozen casserole, covered, at 400° for 1 hour. Uncover; continue baking till heated through, 15 to 20 minutes more. Sprinkle with paprika. Makes 2 casseroles, 4 servings each.

Tuna-Cheese Bake

Three kinds of cheese add flavor—

16 ounces lasagne noodles
 1 cup fresh or frozen chopped onion
 2 cloves garlic, minced
 ¼ cup butter or margarine
 4 6½- or 7-ounce cans tuna, drained
   and flaked
 2 10½-ounce cans condensed cream
   of celery soup
⅔ cup milk
 1 teaspoon dried oregano, crushed
 ¼ teaspoon pepper
 8 slices mozzarella cheese
   (12 ounces)
16 slices process American cheese
   (16 ounces)
 1 cup grated Parmesan cheese

Advance preparation: In large saucepan cook lasagne noodles in boiling salted water according to package directions; drain and set aside. In medium saucepan cook onion and garlic in butter or margarine till onion is tender. Stir in tuna, cream of celery soup, milk, crushed oregano, and pepper. *In each of two 12x7x1½-inch baking dishes, layer one-fourth of the cooked lasagne noodles, half of the tuna mixture, half the mozzarella slices, half the American cheese slices, and half the grated Parmesan cheese.* Top casseroles with remaining lasagne noodles. Cover the casseroles tightly. Seal, label, and freeze up to 2 months.
Before serving: Bake the frozen tuna-cheese casserole, covered, at 400° till it is heated through, about 1½ hours. Makes 2 casseroles, 6 to 8 servings each.

Two for the time of one

Freeze this easy Cauliflower-Tuna Ahoy in a pair → of casseroles. You'll have main dishes ready to launch two meals in the time it took to prepare one.

Read Recipe Before Beginning

Before starting meal preparation, read all recipes through completely, and assemble the utensils and ingredients needed. Also, turn on the oven or broiler to preheat, if necessary. Then, food preparation will not stop while you hunt for a necessary item, but will move smoothly.

Shrimp-Noodle Bake

Keep canned shrimp and cream of shrimp soup on hand for this casserole—

  2 cups medium noodles (about 4 ounces)
  ¼ cup fresh or frozen chopped green pepper
  2 tablespoons butter or margarine
  1 10½-ounce can condensed cream of shrimp soup
  ⅓ cup milk
  1 cup shredded sharp process American cheese (4 ounces)
  2 4½-ounce cans shrimp, drained (1¾ cups)

• • •

  ¾ cup soft bread crumbs (1 slice)
  1 tablespoon butter or margarine, melted

Advance preparation: Cook noodles in boiling salted water till tender but still firm, about 7 minutes. Drain noodles well. Meanwhile, in large saucepan cook chopped green pepper in 2 tablespoons butter or margarine till tender. Stir in cream of shrimp soup and milk; heat, stirring constantly, till bubbly. Add shredded cheese; stir till melted. Stir in drained shrimp and drained noodles. Turn into 1½-quart casserole. Cover; refrigerate up to 24 hours. Toss together soft bread crumbs and 1 tablespoon melted butter or margarine. Wrap and chill.
Before serving: Bake shrimp casserole, covered, at 375° for 30 minutes. Sprinkle crumb mixture atop casserole. Bake, uncovered, till heated through, about 15 minutes longer. Makes 4 or 5 servings.

Ham Croquettes

  3 tablespoons butter or margarine
  3 tablespoons all-purpose flour
  ¾ cup milk
  2 cups ground fully cooked ham (about 10 ounces)
  1 teaspoon instant minced onion
  ½ teaspoon dry mustard
  ¾ cup fine dry bread crumbs
  1 beaten egg
    Fat for frying
  1 8-ounce package frozen peas in cream sauce

Advance preparation: In saucepan melt butter; blend in flour. Add milk; cook and stir till thickened and bubbly. Remove from heat; stir in ham, onion, and dry mustard. Cover; refrigerate up to 24 hours.
Before serving: Shape ham mixture into 8 to 10 balls. Roll in crumbs. Shape into cones, handling lightly. Combine egg and 2 tablespoons water. Dip ham cones into egg mixture. Roll in crumbs again. Fry in deep hot fat (375°) till heated through, about 2 minutes. Drain. Meanwhile, cook peas according to package directions. Serve over croquettes. Makes 4 or 5 servings.

Apricot-Sauced Pork Chops

  ¾ cup orange juice
  ½ cup snipped dried apricots
  ¼ cup sugar
  ¼ teaspoon ground cloves
  6 pork chops, cut ¾ inch thick

Advance preparation: In small saucepan combine juice, apricots, sugar, cloves, and ¼ cup water. Bring to boiling; cover and simmer till apricots are tender, 20 to 25 minutes. Meanwhile, trim fat from pork chops. Heat trimmings till 1 tablespoon fat accumulates; discard trimmings. Brown the chops in hot fat. Sprinkle generously with salt and pepper. Place chops in 11x7½x1½-inch baking pan. Spoon apricot mixture over. Cover; refrigerate up to 24 hours.
Before serving: Bake, covered, at 350° till tender, 45 to 50 minutes. Makes 6 servings.

Pork and Apples with Stuffing

12 pork tenderloin slices (about 4 pounds)
2 20-ounce cans pie-sliced apples, drained
½ cup packed brown sugar
2 teaspoons instant beef bouillon granules
2 cups boiling water
6 cups herb-seasoned stuffing mix
½ cup chopped celery
¼ cup butter or margarine, melted
3 tablespoons instant minced onion
1 teaspoon salt
½ teaspoon ground sage

Advance preparation: Pound tenderloin slices; trim off fat. In large skillet cook trimmings till 2 tablespoons drippings accumulate; discard trimmings. In skillet brown the meat well on both sides. Sprinkle meat with a little salt and pepper. Divide meat between two 12x7½x2-inch baking dishes. Combine apples and brown sugar. Spoon over meat. Dissolve bouillon granules in boiling water. Combine stuffing mix, celery, melted butter, instant onion, salt, and sage; toss with bouillon till moistened. Press stuffing mixture into ½-cup measure; unmold one atop each pork slice. Cover tightly. Seal; label; freeze up to 2 months.
Before serving: Bake frozen casserole, covered, at 400° till pork is done, about 1¼ hours. Makes 2 casseroles, 6 servings each.

Mincemeat Spareribs

Advance preparation: Cut 3 pounds pork spareribs in serving-size pieces. Place ribs in Dutch oven; cover with salted water. Cover pan. Bring to boiling; simmer ribs till almost tender, about 1 hour. Drain; place in shallow baking dish. Combine 1½ cups prepared mincemeat, one 10½-ounce can condensed beef broth, and 2 tablespoons vinegar. Spoon mixture over ribs. Cover; refrigerate up to 24 hours.
Before serving: Bake ribs, uncovered, at 350° for 45 to 55 minutes, spooning sauce over ribs frequently. Makes 4 servings.

Ham and Broccoli Bake

2 10½-ounce cans condensed cream of chicken soup
1 8-ounce jar process cheese spread
½ cup milk
½ cup fresh or frozen chopped onion
¼ cup butter or margarine
2 10-ounce packages frozen chopped broccoli
4 cups diced fully cooked ham
2 cups uncooked packaged precooked rice
½ teaspoon Worcestershire sauce

Advance preparation: Combine soup, cheese spread, and milk. Cook onion in butter till tender. Cook broccoli according to package directions till *almost* tender; drain. Add onion, broccoli, ham, rice, and Worcestershire to soup mixture. Turn into two 1½-quart casseroles. Cover tightly. Seal, label, and freeze up to 2 months.
Before serving: Bake, covered, at 400° for 1½ hours. Uncover; bake 30 minutes more. Makes 2 casseroles, 4 or 5 servings each.

Marinated Beef Tenderloin

½ cup catsup
1 envelope Italian salad dressing mix
1 teaspoon prepared mustard
¼ teaspoon Worcestershire sauce
1 2-pound beef tenderloin

ENTERTAINING SPECIAL

Advance preparation: Combine catsup, dressing mix, mustard, Worcestershire sauce, and ½ cup water. Pierce meat with fork on all sides. Place meat in plastic bag; set in deep bowl. Add marinade to bag; close. Refrigerate 24 hours. Occasionally press bag against meat to distribute marinade.
Before serving: Remove meat from bag, reserving marinade. Roast meat on rack in shallow roasting pan at 425° till desired doneness. Allow about 50 minutes for rare (140°) and about 60 minutes for medium (160°). Baste occasionally with reserved marinade. Heat remaining marinade. Spoon marinade over sliced meat. Serves 6 to 8.

Spaghetti and Meat Rolls

1 beaten egg
¼ cup fresh or frozen chopped onion
2 tablespoons soft bread crumbs
¼ teaspoon salt
⅛ teaspoon pepper
1 pound ground beef
1 8-ounce can tomato sauce
1 cup water
1 8-ounce package Italian dinner
    mix with spaghetti
2 tablespoons fresh or frozen
    chopped onion
2 tablespoons chopped celery
1 tablespoon packed brown sugar
1 tablespoon vinegar

Advance preparation: In bowl combine egg, ¼ cup onion, soft bread crumbs, salt, and pepper. Add ground beef; mix well. Shape into 2 rolls about 6 inches long. Place in 10x6x2-inch baking dish. Combine tomato sauce, water, sauce mix from Italian dinner, 2 tablespoons onion, celery, brown sugar, and vinegar; pour over meat rolls. Cover; refrigerate up to 24 hours.
Before serving: Bake, uncovered, at 350° for 1¼ hours, spooning sauce over meat occasionally. Just before serving, cook spaghetti from dinner mix according to package directions; drain. Turn spaghetti onto serving platter; arrange meat atop and pass sauce. Makes 4 servings.

Basic Ground Beef Mixture

Use this frozen mixture as the base for any of the following four dishes—

2 pounds ground beef
1 cup chopped celery
1 cup fresh or frozen chopped onion
½ cup fresh or frozen chopped green
    pepper

Advance preparation: Cook all ingredients till meat is browned and vegetables are tender. Drain off excess fat. Cool quickly. Divide into three 2-cup portions in moisture-vaporproof containers. Seal, label, and freeze up to 4 months. Makes 6 cups.

Mexican Beef Bake

Tortilla pieces add crunch—

1 16-ounce can tomatoes
1 10-ounce can enchilada sauce
¼ cup sliced pitted ripe olives
1 teaspoon salt
    Dash pepper
2 cups frozen Basic Ground Beef
    Mixture
½ cup cooking oil
8 canned or frozen tortillas
1 cup shredded process American
    cheese (4 ounces)
1 cup cream-style cottage cheese
1 slightly beaten egg

In medium saucepan combine tomatoes, enchilada sauce, ripe olives, salt, and pepper. Add frozen Basic Ground Beef Mixture; simmer, covered, for 20 minutes, stirring occasionally. Heat oil in skillet. Cut *2 tortillas* into quarters. Cook the tortilla quarters and remaining whole tortillas in hot oil till crisp and brown; drain well. Set aside quartered tortillas; break up remaining tortillas. Combine American cheese, cottage cheese, and egg.

Spread *one-third* of the meat mixture in 12x7½x2-inch baking dish. Top with *half* the cheese mixture and *half* the broken tortillas. Repeat layers, ending with meat mixture. Top with quartered tortillas. Bake at 350° for 30 minutes. If desired, sprinkle an additional ½ cup shredded process American cheese over top and return to oven till cheese melts, about 5 minutes more. Let stand 5 minutes before serving. Makes 4 or 5 servings.

Cooling Tip

Do not let foods that need refrigerating stand at room temperature to cool. Since large volumes of hot food can raise the temperature inside the refrigerator or freezer, cool food quickly by placing it in a shallow container and setting this in a pan of ice water.

Slip the refrigerated Spaghetti and Meat Rolls into the oven as soon as you come in the door. You'll have an hour to read the newspaper before cooking the spaghetti and assembling a big tossed green salad.

Hamburger-Corn Casserole

2 cups frozen Basic Ground Beef
   Mixture
1 10¾-ounce can condensed vegetable
   soup
1 10½-ounce can condensed beef broth
1 17-ounce can cream-style corn
½ of a 7-ounce package macaroni
   (1 cup)
2 cups soft bread crumbs (about
   2½ slices bread)
2 tablespoons butter or margarine,
   melted

In saucepan combine frozen beef mixture, soup, and broth. Simmer, covered, for 20 minutes, stirring occasionally. Add corn and uncooked macaroni. Turn into 2-quart casserole. Cover and bake at 375° for 50 minutes. Toss together crumbs and melted butter; sprinkle atop casserole. Bake, uncovered, 10 minutes more. Serves 4 to 6.

Oriental Skillet

2 cups frozen Basic Ground Beef
   Mixture
1 16-ounce can chop suey vegetables,
   drained
1 10-ounce package frozen peas
     • • •
2 tablespoons cornstarch
1 teaspoon sugar
¼ teaspoon ground ginger
3 tablespoons soy sauce
   Chow mein noodles

In large saucepan or skillet combine frozen beef mixture, chop suey vegetables, frozen peas, and 1 cup water. Simmer, covered, for 20 minutes, stirring occasionally. Blend together cornstarch, sugar, and ginger; gradually stir in soy sauce and 2 tablespoons water. Add to beef mixture; cook and stir till thickened and bubbly. Serve over chow mein noodles. Serves 4.

Quick Beef Chowder

    1 16-ounce can tomatoes, cut up
    1 10½-ounce can condensed cream of
        celery soup
    1 8-ounce can whole kernel corn
    2 tablespoons snipped parsley
    2 cups frozen Basic Ground Beef
        Mixture (see recipe, page 12)

In large saucepan stir tomatoes into celery soup; stir in undrained corn, parsley, and ¼ teaspoon salt. Add frozen beef mixture. Simmer, covered, for 20 minutes, stirring occasionally. Makes 4 or 5 servings.

Potato-Topped Stew

    2 tablespoons all-purpose flour
    1 pound beef stew meat, cut in
        ¾-inch cubes
    2 tablespoons shortening
    1 10½-ounce can condensed golden
        mushroom soup
    1 tablespoon instant minced onion
    ¼ teaspoon dried basil, crushed
    1 10-ounce package frozen mixed
        vegetables
    ⅓ cup dry red wine
      Packaged instant mashed potatoes
        (enough for 4 servings)
    ½ cup shredded process American
        cheese (2 ounces)

Advance preparation: Combine flour, 1 teaspoon salt, and dash pepper in plastic or paper bag. Shake meat cubes with flour mixture to coat. In Dutch oven brown the meat in hot shortening. Stir in soup, instant minced onion, basil, and ¾ cup water. Cover; cook, stirring occasionally, for 30 minutes. Add mixed vegetables; continue cooking till meat is tender, about 30 minutes more. Stir in wine. Spoon into 1½-quart casserole. Cover tightly. Seal, label, and freeze up to 2 months.
Before serving: Bake frozen casserole, covered, at 400° for 1¼ hours. Prepare potatoes, following package directions. Spoon around edge; sprinkle with cheese. Bake, uncovered, 15 minutes longer. Serves 4.

Herbed Round Steak

Advance preparation: Using one 2-pound beef round steak cut ¾ inch thick, divide steak into 6 portions. Trim fat. Season meat with ½ teaspoon salt and ⅛ teaspoon pepper. In skillet brown the meat in 2 tablespoons cooking oil; remove meat. In same skillet cook 1 medium onion, sliced, till tender. Return meat to skillet; add ½ cup water. Simmer, covered, for 1 hour. Turn into 12x7½x2-inch baking dish; reserve drippings. Combine one 10½-ounce can condensed cream of celery soup and ¾ cup milk; stir into reserved drippings. Stir in ½ teaspoon dried oregano, crushed, and ¼ teaspoon dried thyme, crushed. Pour over meat. Cover; refrigerate up to 24 hours.
Before serving: Bake, covered, at 350° till heated through, about 1 hour. Serves 6.

Easy Moussaka

Advance preparation: Combine 1 medium eggplant, chopped, and ¼ cup water. Cover; simmer till tender. Turn into 2-quart casserole. In skillet cook 1½ pounds ground beef, ½ cup fresh or frozen chopped onion, and 1 small clove garlic, minced, till beef is browned; drain. Stir in 2 cups finely shredded cabbage, one 8-ounce can tomato sauce, 1 tablespoon Worcestershire sauce, 1 teaspoon salt, ¼ teaspoon pepper, and dash ground nutmeg. Cover; cook 10 minutes. Stir in 1 cup shredded sharp process American cheese. Spoon over eggplant. Cover; refrigerate up to 24 hours.
Before serving: Bake, covered, at 350° for 45 minutes. Uncover; top with ½ cup shredded sharp process American cheese. Bake 15 minutes more. Makes 6 servings.

Make-Ahead Tip

Most casseroles can be refrigerated for as long as 24 hours before baking. Just remember to cover tightly before chilling and allow some extra baking time.

Ravioli Florentine

2 pounds ground beef
1 15-ounce can pizza sauce
2 15-ounce cans spinach
3 cups cream-style cottage cheese
    with chives
2 15-ounce cans ravioli in tomato
    sauce
⅓ cup grated Parmesan cheese

Advance preparation: Brown the beef; drain. Stir in pizza sauce. Drain spinach. In *each* of two 10x6x2-inch baking dishes layer *half* spinach, *one-fourth* meat mixture, *half* cottage cheese, and *half* ravioli. Top with remaining meat mixture. Cover tightly. Seal, label, and freeze up to 2 months.
Before serving: Bake frozen casserole, covered, at 400° for 1¼ hours. Uncover; bake till heated through, about 30 minutes. Sprinkle *each casserole* with about 3 tablespoons Parmesan. Let stand 10 minutes. Makes 2 casseroles, 4 servings each.

Make-Ahead Oriental Beef Stew

1½ pounds beef stew meat, cut in
    1-inch cubes
2 tablespoons cooking oil
½ cup fresh or frozen chopped onion
1 small clove garlic, minced
1 16-ounce can tomatoes
¼ cup soy sauce
½ teaspoon ground ginger
1 large green pepper
2 tablespoons cornstarch

Advance preparation: Brown the beef in hot oil. Add onion, garlic, and 1 cup water. Simmer, covered, for 1¼ hours. Cover; chill. Skim off fat. Spoon meat into freezer container. Seal, label, and freeze.
Before serving: Cut up tomatoes; in saucepan combine with frozen beef, soy, and ginger. Cover. Cook over low heat till thawed and boiling, 20 to 30 minutes; stir often. Cut pepper in strips; add to stew. Simmer, covered, for 5 minutes. Stir in mixture of cornstarch and 2 tablespoons cold water. Cook and stir till bubbly. Serves 4.

Sour Cream Meatballs

1 cup crushed corn chips
1 cup milk
1 clove garlic, minced
3 tablespoons snipped parsley
2 pounds ground beef
3 tablespoons butter or margarine
1 cup fresh or frozen chopped onion
2 tablespoons all-purpose flour
1 10½-ounce can condensed beef broth
1 teaspoon Worcestershire sauce
1 cup dairy sour cream

Advance preparation: Mix first 4 ingredients, 1 teaspoon salt, and ⅛ teaspoon pepper. Mix in beef. Shape into sixty 1-inch balls. Bake in large, shallow baking pan at 375° for 20 minutes; shake pan often to turn meatballs. Cover; chill. In 3-quart saucepan melt butter. Add onion; cook till tender. Blend in flour. Add broth, Worcestershire, and ½ cup water. Cook and stir till bubbly. Cover; refrigerate up to 24 hours.
Before serving: Heat sauce. Add meatballs; heat through. Stir in sour cream. Heat through *(do not boil)*. Serves 6 to 8.

Steak Parisienne

1 beef T-bone steak (about 1½ pounds)
¼ pound fresh mushrooms
5 tablespoons olive oil
½ cup dry red wine
¼ cup red wine vinegar
½ teaspoon lemon pepper seasoning
¼ teaspoon dried thyme, crushed
¼ teaspoon dried basil, crushed
¼ teaspoon dried marjoram, crushed
6 cherry tomatoes
6 canned artichoke hearts

Advance preparation: Broil steak till rare. Chill. Cut into ½-inch slices. Slice mushrooms; cook in *2 tablespoons* oil till just tender. Mix remaining oil, wine, vinegar, seasonings, and 1 teaspoon salt. Pour over meat and mushrooms. Chill 3 hours.
Before serving: Drain meat. Arrange meat, mushrooms, tomatoes, and artichokes on platter. Spoon dressing over. Serves 2 or 3.

Do-Ahead Beef Noodle Bake

4 ounces noodles
1 pound ground beef
½ cup fresh or frozen chopped onion
¼ cup fresh or frozen chopped green
    pepper
1 15-ounce can tomato sauce
½ teaspoon seasoned salt
2 cups cream-style cottage cheese
1 3-ounce package cream cheese,
    softened

Advance preparation: Cook noodles in boiling, salted water till tender. Brown beef, onion, and green pepper; drain off fat. Stir in tomato sauce, seasoned salt, and ¼ teaspoon pepper. Blend cheeses till fluffy. In buttered 10x6x2-inch baking dish layer noodles, cheese mixture, and meat sauce. Cover; refrigerate up to 24 hours.
Before serving: Bake at 350° till heated through, about 40 minutes. Serves 6.

Cheesy Chicken Rolls

4 whole large chicken breasts,
    skinned, boned, and halved
    lengthwise
2 ounces process Swiss cheese, cut
    in 8 strips
2 tablespoons crumbled blue cheese
1 cup fine dry bread crumbs
1 tablespoon butter, melted
    All-purpose flour
2 beaten eggs

Advance preparation: Place chicken pieces, boned side up, between clear plastic wrap. Pound from center out to form cutlets ¼ inch thick. Peel off wrap; sprinkle with salt. Place a strip of Swiss cheese at end of each cutlet; sprinkle with blue cheese. Beginning with short side, roll up jelly-roll fashion, tucking in sides. Press end to seal well. Mix crumbs and butter. Coat each roll with flour; dip in eggs. Roll in crumbs. Place in shallow baking pan. Cover. Refrigerate till well chilled, 1 to 24 hours.
Before serving: Bake, uncovered, at 350° till done, about 45 minutes. Serves 4 to 6.

Chicken Roll-Ups

4 whole medium chicken breasts,
    skinned and boned
2 tablespoons butter, softened
2 tablespoons snipped parsley
⅛ teaspoon dried marjoram, crushed
    All-purpose flour
    Milk
1 2⅜-ounce package seasoned coating
    mix for chicken

Advance preparation: Place chicken breasts, boned side up, between clear plastic wrap. Pound from center out till about ¼ inch thick. Peel off wrap; season with salt. Mix butter, parsley, and marjoram; spread on one side of chicken pieces, spreading not quite to edge. Roll up jelly-roll fashion, tucking in sides. Press seams to seal well. Coat each chicken roll with flour. Dip in milk, then roll in coating mix. Cover lightly; refrigerate up to 24 hours.
Before serving: Bake in shallow baking pan at 400° about 35 minutes. Serves 4.

Individual Chicken Casseroles

½ cup fresh or frozen chopped onion
6 tablespoons butter or margarine
½ cup all-purpose flour
3 cups chicken broth
3 cups cubed cooked chicken
1 10-ounce package frozen peas and
    carrots, cooked and drained
¼ cup chopped canned pimiento

Advance preparation: Cook onion in butter till tender. Blend in flour and 1 teaspoon salt. Stir in chicken broth. Cook and stir till thickened and bubbly. Stir in chicken, peas and carrots, and pimiento. Line 6 to 8 individual casseroles with heavy foil, leaving enough overlapping to seal. Spoon in chicken mixture; seal foil. Freeze. When solid, remove foil packets from casseroles. Label; freeze up to 2 months.
Before serving: Remove foil; set food blocks into casseroles. Bake, covered, at 400° about 1 hour, stirring once or twice toward end of baking time. Serves 6 to 8.

Lazy Paella

    1 3-pound ready-to-cook broiler-
        fryer chicken, cut up
    2 tablespoons cooking oil
    1½ cups chicken broth
    8 ounces shelled shrimp
    1 8½-ounce can peas, drained
    1 6-ounce package saffron rice mix
    1 3-ounce can sliced mushrooms,
        drained
    ½ envelope onion soup mix (¼ cup)

Advance preparation: Brown chicken in oil. Season with salt and pepper. Mix remaining ingredients; spread in 3-quart casserole. Top with chicken. Sprinkle with paprika, if desired. Cover; chill up to 24 hours.
Before serving: Bake, covered, at 350° about 1¼ hours. Makes 4 servings.

Orange Chicken

    ½ cup cooking oil
    ½ teaspoon grated orange peel
    ½ cup orange juice
    1 teaspoon instant minced onion
    ½ teaspoon Worcestershire sauce
    1 2½- to 3-pound ready-to-cook
        broiler-fryer chicken, cut up

Advance preparation: Mix first 5 ingredients and ½ teaspoon salt. Place chicken in plastic bag. Pour oil mixture over. Close bag; place in bowl. Refrigerate 24 hours; press occasionally to distribute marinade.
Before serving: Drain chicken; reserve marinade. Place chicken, skin side down, in broiler pan (no rack). Broil 4 to 5 inches from heat about 40 minutes. Brush often with marinade; turn once. Serves 3 or 4.

Lazy Paella makes a striking entrée for a small company dinner. The chicken-shrimp casserole mixes saffron rice with mushrooms and peas for a brightly decorated main dish. Paprika adds a colorful garnish.

Chicken-Vegetable Strata

Advance preparation: Cook one 8-ounce package frozen mixed vegetables with onion sauce according to package directions. Stir in 1 cup shredded sharp process American cheese, ¾ cup milk, and ½ teaspoon poultry seasoning; cool slightly. Stir in 2 beaten eggs. Cut 3 slices bread in 1-inch cubes. Place *half* bread in 10x6x2-inch baking dish. Top with 1½ cups cubed cooked chicken, then remaining bread. Pour vegetable mixture over. Cover; refrigerate up to 24 hours. Toss 1 cup soft bread crumbs with 2 tablespoons butter, melted. Wrap; chill.

Before serving: Sprinkle crumbs atop casserole. Bake, uncovered, at 325° till set, 50 to 60 minutes. Let stand 10 minutes before serving. Makes 4 to 6 servings.

Chicken and Rice Balls

　½ cup chopped celery
　¼ cup sliced green onion
　2 tablespoons butter or margarine
　2 tablespoons all-purpose flour
　¼ cup chicken broth
　2 cups cooked short grain rice
　1½ cups diced cooked chicken
　½ cup shredded process
　　　American cheese (2 ounces)
　1 beaten egg
　½ teaspoon poultry seasoning
　½ cup cornflake crumbs
　1 10¾-ounce can condensed cream
　　　of mushroom soup
　⅓ cup milk
　2 tablespoons sliced green onion

Advance preparation: Cook celery and ¼ cup onion in butter till tender. Blend in flour; add broth. Cook and stir till thick. Stir in next 5 ingredients and ½ teaspoon salt. Shape mixture into 12 balls; roll in crumbs. Place in 13x9x2-inch baking pan. Cover; refrigerate up to 24 hours.

Before serving: Bake, uncovered, at 350° for 35 to 40 minutes. Meanwhile, for sauce combine soup, milk, and 2 tablespoons onion; heat through. Serve sauce over chicken balls. Makes 4 servings.

Chicken-Noodle Dinner

　2 envelopes chicken-noodle soup mix
　1 6-ounce can sliced mushrooms
　2 6-ounce cans evaporated milk
　½ cup butter or margarine
　½ cup all-purpose flour
　1 10-ounce package frozen mixed
　　　vegetables
　4 cups diced cooked chicken
　4 eggs

Advance preparation: In saucepan combine soup mix and 3 cups water; bring to boiling. Reduce heat; cover and simmer 5 minutes. Strain, reserving broth. Divide noodles in half; freeze in two packages. Drain mushrooms, reserving liquid. Combine reserved broth, mushroom liquid, and evaporated milk. In saucepan melt butter or margarine; blend in flour, ½ teaspoon salt, and ¼ teaspoon pepper. Add broth mixture; cook and stir till thickened. Break up frozen vegetables with fork; add to broth mixture along with mushrooms and chicken. Turn into two 1½-quart casseroles. Cover tightly. Seal, label, and freeze up to 2 months.

Before serving: Bake frozen casserole, covered, at 400° for 1¼ hours; stir once or twice. *For each casserole,* beat 2 eggs; combine eggs, one package of the frozen noodles, and ¼ teaspoon salt. Spoon atop casserole. Bake, covered, 10 minutes more. Makes 2 casseroles, 6 to 8 servings each.

Stuffed Baked Franks

Advance preparation: Slit 5 or 6 large frankfurters (1 pound) lengthwise almost to opposite side. Cook ¼ cup minced onion in 1 tablespoon butter till tender. Mix 2 cups herb-seasoned stuffing mix, the onion, ¾ cup water, ¼ cup catsup, and 1 tablespoon sweet pickle relish. Mound stuffing into slit franks. Place on baking sheet. Cover; refrigerate up to 24 hours.

Before serving: Bake at 400° for 10 to 15 minutes. Cut 3 slices sharp process American cheese into strips. Top franks with cheese strips; bake till cheese melts, about 3 minutes. Makes 5 or 6 servings.

Frankfurter-Cheese Casserole

Advance preparation: Cook ¾ cup maca-roni in boiling salted water till tender, about 8 minutes; drain well. Cook ⅓ cup fresh or frozen chopped onion and ⅓ cup fresh or frozen chopped green pepper in 2 table-spoons butter till tender. Blend in 3 table-spoons all-purpose flour and 1 teaspoon *each* Worcestershire sauce and prepared mustard. Add 1 cup milk. Cook and stir till thickened and bubbly. Stir in macaroni, 1½ cups cream-style cottage cheese, and 6 frankfurters, thinly sliced. Turn into 1½-quart casserole. Cover; refrigerate up to 24 hours. Toss 1½ cups soft bread crumbs and 2 tablespoons butter, melted. Wrap; chill.
Before serving: Bake casserole, covered, at 350° for 40 minutes, gently stirring occasionally. Sprinkle crumbs on top. Bake, uncovered, till heated through, about 10 minutes more. Let stand 5 to 10 minutes before serving. Makes 4 to 6 servings.

Western Baked Beans

Arrange Polish sausages in a pinwheel atop—

>   4 slices bacon
>   1 cup fresh or frozen chopped onion
>   1 clove garlic, minced
>   1 16-ounce can kidney beans, drained
>   1 16-ounce can lima beans, drained
>   1 16-ounce can butter beans, drained
>   1 14-ounce jar baked beans in
>   molasses sauce
>   ½ cup catsup
>   ½ cup dry red wine
>   3 tablespoons packed brown sugar
>   ½ teaspoon dry mustard
>   6 Polish sausages, halved diagonally

Advance preparation: Cook bacon till crisp; remove and crumble. Cook onion and garlic in bacon drippings till onion is tender. Com-bine onion, garlic, beans, catsup, wine, brown sugar, dry mustard, bacon, and ¼ teaspoon pepper. Spoon into 3-quart casse-role. Cover; refrigerate up to 24 hours.
Before serving: Arrange sausages atop beans. Bake, uncovered, at 375° till heated through, about 1 hour. Makes 6 servings.

Sausage Lasagne

>   4 ounces lasagne noodles
>   ½ pound Italian sausage
>   1 8-ounce can tomatoes
>   1 8-ounce can tomato sauce with
>   onion
>   ¼ teaspoon dried oregano, crushed
>   1 beaten egg
>   1½ cups fresh ricotta *or* cream-style
>   cottage cheese
>   ¼ cup grated Parmesan cheese
>   1½ teaspoons dried parsley flakes
>   1 6-ounce package sliced mozzarella
>   cheese

Advance preparation: Cook noodles ac-cording to package directions; drain. Cook sausage till browned; drain off fat. Mix sausage, tomatoes, tomato sauce, and oreg-ano. Mix egg, ricotta or cottage cheese, Par-mesan, and parsley. Place *half* noodles in 10x6x2-inch baking dish. Spread with *half* cheese mixture; top with *half* mozzarella. Cover with *half* sausage mixture. Repeat layers. Cover; refrigerate up to 24 hours.
Before serving: Bake, covered, at 375° about 50 minutes. Let stand 10 minutes. Serves 6.

Tangy Lamb Shoulder Chops

>   4 lamb shoulder chops, cut ¾ inch
>   thick (about 2 pounds)
>   1 tablespoon shortening
>   ¼ cup hot-style catsup
>   1 teaspoon dried basil, crushed
>   4 onion slices
>   4 green pepper rings
>   ¼ cup shredded process American
>   cheese (1 ounce)

Advance preparation: Trim excess fat from chops. Brown the chops in hot shortening. Sprinkle with ½ teaspoon salt and dash pepper. Place in 9x9x2-inch baking dish. Spread with catsup; sprinkle with basil. Top with onion and green pepper. Cover; refrigerate up to 24 hours.
Before serving: Bake, covered, at 350° about 1 hour. Uncover; sprinkle cheese inside peppers. Bake till cheese melts. Serves 4.

Serve hearty Stroganoff Steak Sandwiches *with mugs of beer for a man-pleasing supper. The meat gets its unusual flavor from a beer marinade. French bread, onions, and a sour cream topper complete the sandwich.*

Ham Loaf Sandwiches

2 beaten eggs
½ cup coarsely crushed saltine
    crackers (10 crackers)
½ cup milk
¼ cup packed brown sugar
2 tablespoons vinegar
1 tablespoon prepared mustard
1½ pounds fully cooked ham, ground
    (about 5 cups)
½ pound ground pork
    Sliced rye bread
    Sweet pickle relish

Advance preparation: Combine eggs, crushed crackers, milk, brown sugar, vinegar, mustard, and dash pepper; mix in ham and pork. Pat into 9x5x3-inch loaf pan. Bake at 350° about 1¼ hours. Drain off fat. Refrigerate in pan till well chilled.
Before serving: Slice loaf. Serve on rye bread with sweet pickle relish and additional mustard. Makes 6 to 8 sandwiches.

Tuna-Cabbage Buns

Pack Cheddar cheese sticks and potato chips in the lunch box with this tasty sandwich—

1 cup chopped cabbage
1 6½- or 7-ounce can tuna, drained
    and flaked
⅓ cup mayonnaise or salad dressing
2 tablespoons chopped green onion
    with tops
      • • •
    Butter or margarine, softened
4 hamburger buns, split

Advance preparation: In small mixing bowl combine chopped cabbage, flaked tuna, mayonnaise or salad dressing, and chopped green onion with tops; mix well. Cover; refrigerate up to 24 hours.
Before serving: Spread butter on bottom halves of hamburger buns. Spread with tuna mixture. Cover with top halves of hamburger buns. Garnish sandwiches with pickle slices, if desired. Makes 4 sandwiches.

Shrimpwich

A hearty sandwich for one or two—

1 4½-ounce can small shrimp, drained
1 hard-cooked egg, chopped
¼ cup mayonnaise or salad dressing
1 tablespoon chili sauce
½ teaspoon instant minced onion
1 individual French roll
   Lettuce

Advance preparation: In small bowl combine shrimp, egg, mayonnaise or salad dressing, chili sauce, and instant minced onion. Cover tightly; chill up to 24 hours.
Before serving: Cut thin slice from top of roll; hollow out. Fill roll with shrimp mixture. Add lettuce. Makes 1 sandwich.

Stroganoff Steak Sandwiches

⅔ cup beer
⅓ cup cooking oil
1 teaspoon salt
¼ teaspoon garlic powder
¼ teaspoon pepper
2 pounds beef flank steak, cut
   1 inch thick
2 tablespoons butter or margarine
½ teaspoon paprika
4 cups sliced onion
12 slices French bread, toasted
1 cup dairy sour cream
½ teaspoon prepared horseradish

Advance preparation: Combine beer, oil, salt, garlic powder, and pepper. Pour into shallow dish. Place steak in beer mixture. Cover and marinate overnight in refrigerator.
Before serving: Drain steak; pat dry with paper toweling. Broil steak 3 inches from heat till desired doneness. (Allow 5 to 7 minutes on each side for medium-rare.) Melt butter; blend in paprika and dash salt. Add onion; cook till tender. Thinly slice meat on the diagonal across grain. *For each sandwich,* arrange meat over 2 slices bread. Top with onions. Warm sour cream; stir in horseradish and spoon over onions. Sprinkle with additional paprika, if desired. Makes 6 sandwiches.

Freezing Sandwiches

Keep frozen sandwiches on hand for lunches or simple suppers. Make several sandwiches at once and then store them in the freezer for up to 2 weeks.

Sandwich fillings that freeze well include cream cheese, hard-cooked egg yolks, sliced or ground cooked meat and poultry, tuna, salmon, and peanut butter. *Do not freeze* sandwiches containing lettuce, celery, tomatoes, cucumbers, egg whites, jelly, or mayonnaise.

Greek-Style Sandwiches

Colorful sandwiches shown on page 2—

½ cup dry red wine
2 tablespoons olive or cooking oil
1 small clove garlic, minced
½ teaspoon dried oregano, crushed
½ teaspoon salt
   Dash freshly ground pepper
1 pound beef sirloin steak,
   cut ½ inch thick
1 tablespoon butter
4 or 5 Bread Envelopes
   (see recipe, page 22)
2 cups chopped lettuce
1 cup diced, seeded tomato (1 large)
⅔ cup diced, seeded cucumber (about
   1 small)
1 cup sour cream dip with chives

Advance preparation: Combine wine, oil, garlic, oregano, salt, and pepper. Cut steak into strips, 2 inches long and ¼ inch wide. Pour wine mixture over beef strips. Cover; refrigerate up to 24 hours.
Before serving: Drain beef strips well. In medium skillet cook *half* the meat in hot butter, stirring to brown on all sides, 2 to 3 minutes. Repeat with remaining meat strips. With sharp knife, open one side of each thawed Bread Envelope to make a pocket. Fill pocket with cooked meat strips, chopped lettuce, diced tomato, diced cucumber, and sour cream dip with chives. Makes 4 or 5 sandwiches.

Bread Envelopes

Use these for Greek-Style Sandwiches (page 21) —

Advance preparation: In large mixer bowl soften 1 package active dry yeast in 1¼ cups warm water (110°). Add 2 cups all-purpose flour, ¼ cup shortening, and 1½ teaspoons salt. Beat at low speed of electric mixer for ½ minute, scraping bowl. Beat 3 minutes at high speed. Stir in 1¼ to 1½ cups flour to make a soft dough. Turn out onto lightly floured surface. Knead 4 to 5 minutes. Cover; let rest in warm place about 15 minutes. Divide into 12 equal pieces. Roll between floured hands into very smooth balls. Cover with plastic wrap or a damp cloth; let rest 10 minutes. Using fingers, gently flatten balls without creasing dough. Cover; let rest 10 minutes. (Keep covered till ready to use.)

Lightly roll one piece at a time on well floured surface to a 7-inch round; *turn dough over once.* Do not stretch, puncture, or crease dough. Be sure to work with enough flour so dough does not stick. Bake, two at a time, on baking sheet at 450° till puffed and softly set, about 3 minutes. Turn over; bake till starts to brown, about 2 minutes more. Cool about 10 minutes; wrap. Label and freeze. Repeat; rolling and baking one batch at a time. Makes 12.

Salad Burgers

Relish-topped sandwiches shown on the cover —

    ¼ cup vinegar
    2 tablespoons sugar
    1 cup chopped onion
    1 large tomato, diced
    ½ medium cucumber, thinly sliced
    2 pounds ground beef
    8 hamburger buns, split and toasted

Advance preparation: Mix vinegar, sugar, ¼ cup water, 1 teaspoon salt, and ⅛ teaspoon pepper. Add vegetables. Cover; chill.
Before serving: Mix meat, 1½ teaspoons salt, and ⅛ teaspoon pepper; shape into 8 patties. Broil 3 inches from heat till done, about 10 minutes, turning once. Place on bottoms of buns. Drain vegetable mixture; spoon onto patties. Add bun tops. Serves 8.

Horseradish-Sauced Beefwiches

Advance preparation: In saucepan combine 2 beaten egg yolks, 2 tablespoons freshly grated horseradish, 2 tablespoons vinegar, 1 tablespoon sugar, 1 tablespoon prepared mustard, 1 tablespoon water, and ½ teaspoon salt. Mix well. Cook and stir over low heat till thickened, about 2 minutes. Remove from heat. Stir till smooth. Refrigerate till well chilled, 3 to 24 hours.
Before serving: Whip ½ cup whipping cream; fold into chilled horseradish mixture. Assemble sandwiches of buttered rye bread, lettuce, and sliced, chilled cooked roast beef. Top with dollops of horseradish mixture. Makes about 1⅓ cups sauce.

Sweet-Sour Chicken Mold

    2 packages sour cream sauce mix
        (each enough for 1 cup sauce)
    2 3-ounce packages lemon-flavored
        gelatin
    2 cups boiling water
    ½ cup cold water
    2 tablespoons lemon juice
    1 teaspoon dried dillweed
    1 medium green pepper, seeded and
        quartered
    1 medium cucumber, peeled,
        quartered, and seeded
    1 small carrot, sliced
    2 5-ounce cans boned chicken,
        drained and cut up
    Assorted fresh vegetables

ENTERTAINING SPECIAL

Advance preparation: Prepare sauce mix according to package directions (including letting stand 10 minutes). Dissolve gelatin in boiling water; add sour cream sauce, cold water, lemon juice, and dillweed. Beat till blended. Chill till partially set. Place green pepper, cucumber, and carrot in blender container; cover with *cold* water. Cover; blend just till coarsely chopped. Drain well; stir chopped vegetables and chicken into gelatin mixture. Turn into 7½-cup ring mold. Chill till firm.
Before serving: Unmold and fill center with fresh vegetables. Makes 8 servings.

Chicken-Raspberry Salad

Advance preparation: Sieve one 10-ounce package frozen raspberries, thawed, by pushing through strainer. Add enough water to make 1 cup liquid. In saucepan combine ⅓ cup sugar, 1 envelope unflavored gelatin, and dash salt. Stir in raspberry mixture. Heat and stir till gelatin dissolves. Stir in ½ cup cold water and 3 tablespoons lemon juice. Chill till partially set. Fold in 1 cup small cantaloupe balls. Pour into 3½-cup ring mold. Chill till firm. Combine 1½ cups cubed cooked chicken, ½ cup diced celery, ⅓ cup mayonnaise, 2 tablespoons chopped sweet pickle, and ¼ teaspoon salt. Toss lightly. Cover; chill up to 24 hours.
Before serving: Unmold gelatin and fill center with chicken mixture. Serves 4.

Ham-Rice Salad

1 10-ounce package frozen rice pilaf
¼ cup mayonnaise or salad dressing
2 teaspoons vinegar
½ teaspoon curry powder
1 cup cubed fully cooked ham
1 medium apple, chopped (1 cup)
• • •
Lettuce cups

Advance preparation: Cook rice pilaf according to package directions; cool. In mixing bowl stir together mayonnaise or salad dressing, vinegar, and curry powder. Add cooked rice pilaf, ham, and apple. Cover; refrigerate up to 24 hours.
Before serving: Spoon chilled salad mixture into lettuce cups. Makes 4 servings.

Sour cream sauce mix, lemon juice, and dillweed combine with lemon-flavored gelatin to produce the distinctive flavors in Sweet-Sour Chicken Mold. *To serve, fill the center with an assortment of crisp, fresh vegetables.*

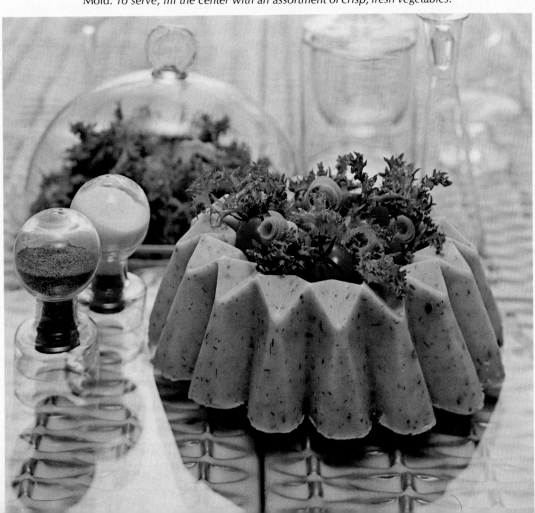

Macaroni-Frank Salad

Advance preparation: Cook 2 cups macaroni in boiling, salted water till tender. Drain. Pour ½ cup Italian salad dressing over macaroni; refrigerate at least 4 hours. Stir in 2 cups diced celery; 4 or 5 frankfurters, thinly sliced; ¼ cup finely snipped parsley; and ¼ cup sweet pickle relish. Stir in ½ cup dairy sour cream. Refrigerate up to 24 hours. Makes 6 servings.

Beef Supper Salad

⅓ cup mayonnaise or salad dressing
¼ cup chili sauce
1 tablespoon sweet pickle relish
2 cups cubed cooked beef
1 8-ounce can kidney beans, drained
1 cup sliced celery
½ cup chopped onion
2 hard-cooked eggs, chopped

Advance preparation: Combine first 3 ingredients, ½ teaspoon salt, and dash pepper. Combine beef, beans, celery, onion, and eggs. Pour dressing over bean mixture; toss lightly. Refrigerate up to 24 hours. Stir before serving. Serves 4 or 5.

Fruited Chicken Salad

1 8-ounce can jellied cranberry
    sauce, chilled
1 13¼-ounce can pineapple tidbits
½ cup dairy sour cream
1 3-ounce package cream cheese,
    softened
1½ cups cubed cooked chicken
¾ cup sliced celery
½ cup chopped walnuts
2 tablespoons chopped green pepper

Advance preparation: Cut cranberry sauce into cubes; chill. Drain pineapple. Beat together sour cream, cheese, and dash salt. Fold in chicken, pineapple, celery, nuts, and green pepper. Refrigerate up to 24 hours. **Before serving:** Top chicken mixture with cranberry cubes. Makes 4 or 5 servings.

Chicken-Wild Rice Salad

1 6-ounce package long grain and
    wild rice mix
2 cups cubed cooked chicken
¼ cup chopped green pepper
2 tablespoons chopped canned
    pimiento
½ cup mayonnaise or salad dressing
2 tablespoons Russian salad dressing
1 tablespoon lemon juice
¼ teaspoon salt
1 or 2 avocados

Advance preparation: Cook rice mix according to package directions; cool. Combine chicken, green pepper, and pimiento. Stir in rice. Mix mayonnaise, Russian dressing, juice, and ¼ teaspoon salt; toss with rice mixture. Refrigerate up to 24 hours. **Before serving:** Peel and slice avocados. Spoon salad over slices. Serves 4 to 6.

Shrimp-Tomato Vinaigrette

4 tomatoes
1 pound fresh or frozen shelled
    shrimp, cooked (2 cups)
1 6-ounce package frozen pea pods,
    thawed and drained
2 tablespoons sliced green onion
    with tops
½ cup salad oil
¼ cup dry white wine
¼ cup wine vinegar
1 envelope Italian salad dressing
    mix
1 to 2 tablespoons capers, well
    drained

Advance preparation: With stem ends down cut tomatoes into wedges, *cutting to, but not through base.* Spread wedges apart slightly; salt lightly. Cover; chill. Combine shrimp, pea pods, and onion. Mix remaining ingredients and dash pepper; pour over shrimp mixture. Cover; chill several hours. **Before serving:** Drain shrimp mixture, reserving marinade. Spoon mixture into tomato shells on serving plate. Pass remaining marinade, if desired. Serves 4.

Chef's Rice Salad

Advance preparation: Bring 1½ cups water and ½ teaspoon salt to boiling. Add one 10-ounce package frozen peas. Return to boil; cook 2 minutes. Stir in 1 cup uncooked packaged precooked rice; cover. Remove from heat; let stand 5 minutes. Stir in ¾ cup mayonnaise, ¼ cup chopped dill pickle, 1 teaspoon grated onion, and dash pepper. Refrigerate up to 24 hours.

Before serving: Spoon rice mixture onto lettuce-lined plates. Top with *half* of a 12-ounce can chopped ham, cut in thin strips, and ½ cup Swiss cheese cut in thin strips (2 ounces). Makes 4 or 5 servings.

Cranberry-Tuna Salad Mold

    1 3-ounce package lemon-flavored
        gelatin
    ½ cup orange juice
    1 16-ounce can jellied cranberry
        sauce
    2 or 3 drops red food coloring
    1 6½- or 7-ounce can tuna, drained
        and flaked
    ½ cup chopped celery
    1 hard-cooked egg, chopped
    ¼ cup sliced pimiento-stuffed green
        olives
    1 tablespoon finely chopped onion
    1 cup mayonnaise or salad dressing
    ½ teaspoon salt
        Dash pepper
    1 envelope unflavored gelatin

Advance preparation: In saucepan combine lemon-flavored gelatin, orange juice, and ½ cup water; cook and stir till boiling and gelatin dissolves. Beat jellied cranberry sauce and red food coloring till smooth; stir into gelatin mixture. Turn into 6½-cup mold. Chill till almost firm.

Combine tuna, celery, egg, olives, and onion. Fold in mayonnaise, salt, and dash pepper. Soften unflavored gelatin in ½ cup cold water; heat and stir till dissolved. Stir into tuna mixture. Chill till partially set; spoon over cranberry layer. Chill till firm. Makes 5 or 6 servings.

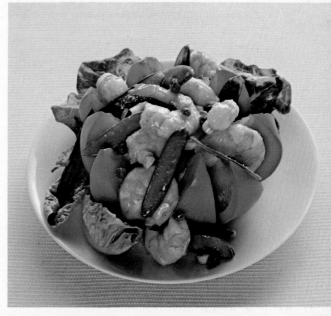

Weary appetites perk up at the sight of Shrimp-Tomato Vinaigrette. This marinated main dish salad will become a favorite for hot-weather meals.

Macaroni-Shrimp Salad

    ¾ cup small macaroni shells
    8 ounces fresh or frozen shelled
        shrimp, cooked and cut in half
        lengthwise
    ⅓ cup chopped celery
    2 tablespoons sliced pimiento-
        stuffed green olives
    1 tablespoon snipped parsley
    ½ cup mayonnaise or salad dressing
    2 tablespoons red wine vinegar
    2 teaspoons lemon juice
    ¼ teaspoon garlic salt
    ¼ teaspoon dry mustard
    ¼ teaspoon paprika

Advance preparation: Cook macaroni in boiling salted water till tender; drain. Combine macaroni, shrimp, celery, olives, and parsley. Blend together mayonnaise, wine vinegar, lemon juice, garlic salt, mustard, and paprika; toss with shrimp mixture. Refrigerate up to 24 hours. Serves 4.

Side Dishes and Desserts

Horseradish Bloody Mary

A perfect meal-starter—

Advance preparation: In large pitcher combine one 46-ounce can tomato juice, 2 cups vodka, 2 tablespoons lemon juice, 1 tablespoon prepared horseradish, 1 teaspoon Worcestershire sauce, ¾ teaspoon salt, and few drops bottled hot pepper sauce. Refrigerate several hours or overnight.
Before serving: Pour mixture over ice. Use celery stick stirrers. Makes 2 quarts.

Cream of Avocado Soup

2 large avocados, peeled
    and mashed
2 cups light cream
1 13¾-ounce can chicken broth
1 tablespoon lemon juice

Advance preparation: In blender container combine all ingredients, ½ teaspoon salt, and dash pepper. Cover; blend till smooth. Refrigerate 5 to 24 hours.
Before serving: If desired, garnish each serving with dried dillweed. Serves 8 to 10.

Festive Cheese Ball

2 5-ounce jars process cheese spread
    with smoke flavor
2 3-ounce packages cream cheese
1 5-ounce jar sharp process
    American cheese spread
2 teaspoons grated onion
½ teaspoon Worcestershire sauce
½ cup snipped parsley
    Assorted crackers

Advance preparation: In small mixer bowl combine first 5 ingredients; beat with electric mixer till smooth. Shape into a ball. Roll in parsley. Refrigerate up to 24 hours. Serve with crackers.

Tomato-Cucumber Marinade

2 medium tomatoes, sliced
1 medium cucumber, peeled and
    thinly sliced (1¼ cups)
½ medium onion, thinly sliced and
    separated into rings (1 cup)
• • •
½ cup salad oil
¼ cup vinegar
1 teaspoon salt
1 teaspoon dried basil, crushed
1 teaspoon dried tarragon, crushed
⅛ teaspoon pepper
    Lettuce

Advance preparation: Layer tomatoes, cucumber, and onion in shallow glass dish. Combine oil, vinegar, salt, basil, tarragon, and pepper; beat well with rotary or electric beater. Pour mixture over vegetables. Cover; refrigerate for 5 to 24 hours.
Before serving: Drain vegetables, reserving marinade. Arrange marinated vegetables in lettuce-lined bowl. Pass reserved marinade. Makes 6 servings.

Citrus Dressing

Advance preparation: In saucepan combine 1 beaten egg; *half* of a 6-ounce can frozen grapefruit-orange juice concentrate, thawed (⅓ cup); ¼ cup water; and 3 tablespoons sugar. Cook and stir over low heat till thickened. Chill. Fold in ½ cup frozen whipped dessert topping, thawed, and ¼ cup mayonnaise. Refrigerate up to 24 hours. Serve over fruit salads. Makes 1½ cups.

Mealmates that wait

Serve make-ahead Tomato-Cucumber Marinade, →
Fruited Granola *(see recipe, page 29), and* Layered
Gelatin Parfaits *(see recipe, page 30) frequently.*

Lemon-Blueberry Salad

1 3-ounce package lemon-
flavored gelatin
1 3-ounce package black raspberry-
flavored gelatin
1 cup boiling water
1 tablespoon lemon juice
1 21-ounce can blueberry pie filling
1 cup dairy sour cream
¼ cup sifted powdered sugar

Advance preparation: Dissolve gelatins in boiling water; add juice and ½ cup cold water. Gradually stir into pie filling. Pour into 8x8x2-inch dish; chill till firm. Blend sour cream and sugar. Spread over gelatin. Chill. Serves 8 or 9.

Cottage Cheese-Cucumber Salad

Refreshing salad shown on the cover—

1 3-ounce package lemon-flavored
gelatin
1 cup boiling water
2 tablespoons lemon juice
1 teaspoon grated onion
1 cup cream-style cottage cheese,
drained
1 cup finely chopped cucumber

Advance preparation: Dissolve gelatin in water. Add juice and onion. Chill till partially set. Beat till light and fluffy. Fold in cheese and cucumber. Pour into individual molds; chill till firm. Serves 6.

Cottage Potato Salad

Advance preparation: Combine 2 cups cubed cooked potatoes and 2 hard-cooked eggs, chopped. Combine ¼ cup dairy sour cream and 2 tablespoons Italian salad dressing; toss with potato mixture. Combine 2 cups cream-style cottage cheese, ½ cup chopped celery, ⅓ cup sliced radishes, ⅓ cup sliced pitted ripe olives, 3 tablespoons thinly sliced green onion, and ½ teaspoon salt. Toss with potato mixture; pack into 5½-cup ring mold. Chill well. Serves 8.

Spicy Fruit Salad

This attractive salad is shown on page 81—

1 8¾-ounce can pineapple tidbits
1 8½-ounce can pear halves
2 tablespoons lemon juice
2 inches stick cinnamon
6 whole cloves
1 orange, peeled and sectioned
Lettuce

Advance preparation: In medium saucepan combine undrained pineapple tidbits, undrained pear halves, and lemon juice. Tie stick cinnamon and whole cloves in cheesecloth bag; add to fruit mixture. Bring mixture to a boil. Reduce heat; cover and simmer 8 to 10 minutes, stirring occasionally. Remove from heat. Add orange sections. Cover; refrigerate several hours or overnight, stirring occasionally.
Before serving: Drain fruit mixture. Remove and discard spice bag. Arrange fruit on lettuce-lined plates. Makes 4 servings.

Orange Perfection Salad

Cabbage and celery add crunch—

1 3-ounce package lemon-flavored
gelatin
2 tablespoons sugar
¼ teaspoon salt
1 cup boiling water
½ cup cold water
½ cup orange juice
1 tablespoon vinegar
1 orange, peeled, sectioned, and
diced
1 cup shredded cabbage
¼ cup finely chopped celery
Lettuce

Advance preparation: Dissolve lemon-flavored gelatin, sugar, and salt in boiling water. Add cold water, orange juice, and vinegar; chill till partially set. Fold in diced orange, shredded cabbage, and celery; turn into 3½-cup mold. Chill till firm.
Before serving: Unmold onto lettuce-lined plate. Trim with an orange twist, if desired. Makes 6 servings.

Succotash Bake

3 tablespoons all-purpose flour
1 8-ounce can cream-style corn
1 3-ounce package cream cheese with chives
1 16-ounce can lima beans, drained
½ cup shredded process American cheese
1½ cups soft bread crumbs
2 tablespoons butter or margarine, melted

Advance preparation: In saucepan stir flour into cream-style corn. Add cream cheese with chives; heat and stir till cheese melts and mixture thickens and bubbles. Stir in lima beans and shredded American cheese. Pour into 1-quart casserole. Cover; refrigerate up to 24 hours. Toss bread crumbs with melted butter; wrap and chill.
Before serving: Bake, covered, at 400° for 30 minutes. Top with crumbs. Bake, uncovered, 20 minutes more. Serves 6.

Broccoli-Blue Cheese Casserole

2 10-ounce packages frozen chopped broccoli
2 tablespoons butter or margarine
2 tablespoons all-purpose flour
1 3-ounce package cream cheese, softened
2 tablespoons crumbled blue cheese
1 cup milk
½ cup crushed rich round crackers
2 tablespoons butter or margarine, melted

Advance preparation: Cook broccoli according to package directions; drain well. In saucepan melt 2 tablespoons butter; stir in flour. Stir in cream cheese and blue cheese. Add milk; cook and stir till bubbly. Stir in broccoli. Pour into 1-quart casserole. Cover; refrigerate up to 24 hours. Toss crushed crackers with 2 tablespoons melted butter; wrap and chill.
Before serving: Top casserole with crumbs. Bake, covered, at 350° for 45 minutes. Uncover; bake 5 to 10 minutes more. Serves 6.

Fruited Granola

Breakfast or snack treat shown on page 27 —

1½ cups quick-cooking rolled oats
1 cup coarsely chopped raw peanuts
1 cup grape nuts cereal
1 cup snipped mixed dried fruit
¼ cup packed brown sugar

Advance preparation: Combine rolled oats, chopped raw peanuts, and cereal. Spread in 15½x10½x1-inch baking pan. Bake at 400° for 10 minutes, stirring once. Stir in dried fruit and brown sugar. Store in tightly covered container. Serve with milk, if desired. Makes about 4½ cups.

Brown-and-Serve Potato Rolls

5 to 5¼ cups all-purpose flour
1 envelope active dry yeast
½ cup mashed cooked potatoes
⅓ cup cooking oil
¼ cup sugar

Advance preparation: In large mixer bowl combine *2 cups* of the flour and the yeast. Combine mashed potatoes, oil, sugar, 1½ cups warm water (110°), and 1 teaspoon salt. Add to dry ingredients in mixer bowl. Beat at low speed of electric mixer for ½ minute, scraping sides of bowl constantly. Beat 3 minutes at high speed. By hand, stir in enough of the remaining flour to make a moderately stiff dough.

Turn out on lightly floured surface; knead till smooth, 5 to 8 minutes. Shape into ball. Place in greased bowl; turn once. Cover; let rise in warm place till almost double (45 to 60 minutes). Punch down; turn out on lightly floured surface. Cover; let rest 10 minutes. Shape into 24 rolls. Place on greased baking sheet or in greased muffin pans. Cover; let rise till almost double (30 to 40 minutes). Bake at 325° for 10 to 12 minutes; *do not brown.* Remove from pan; cool. Wrap; freeze.
Before serving: Unwrap slightly. Thaw at room temperature 10 to 15 minutes. Unwrap. Bake on ungreased baking sheet at 450° till golden, 5 to 10 minutes. Makes 24.

Blueberry-Orange Nut Bread

   3 cups all-purpose flour
   ¾ cup sugar
   3 teaspoons baking powder
   ¼ teaspoon baking soda
   3 eggs
   ½ cup milk
   ½ cup butter or margarine, melted
   1 tablespoon grated orange peel
   ⅔ cup orange juice
   1 cup fresh, frozen, or drained,
      canned blueberries
   ½ cup chopped walnuts

Advance preparation: In mixing bowl stir flour, sugar, baking powder, soda, and 1 teaspoon salt together thoroughly. Beat together eggs, milk, butter, peel, and juice; stir into dry ingredients just till moistened. Fold in berries and nuts. Pour into greased 9x5x3-inch loaf pan. Bake at 350° for 60 to 70 minutes. Remove from pan; cool well. Wrap in foil and store overnight before slicing. Makes 1 loaf.

Layered Gelatin Parfaits

These special parfaits are shown on page 27—

   1 3-ounce package lemon-flavored
      gelatin
   1 cup boiling water
   1 10-ounce package frozen
      mixed fruit
   ½ cup lemon yogurt
   2 teaspoons sugar

Advanced preparation: Dissolve gelatin and dash salt in boiling water; stir in ¾ cup cold water. Set aside ½ cup mixture. Add frozen fruit to remaining gelatin mixture, stirring carefully to separate fruits. Chill till partially set, 10 to 15 minutes; spoon into 6 parfait glasses. Chill till almost set. Meanwhile, chill the reserved ½ cup gelatin till partially set. Beat with rotary or electric beater till light and fluffy, 1 to 2 minutes. Blend lemon yogurt and sugar; fold into whipped gelatin. Spoon whipped gelatin mixture atop gelatin in parfait glasses. Chill till set. Makes 6 servings.

Chocolate Surprise Cake

   1 10-inch angel cake
  32 large marshmallows
   ⅓ cup water
   ¼ teaspoon salt
   1 6-ounce package semisweet
      chocolate pieces (1 cup)
   ¼ teaspoon vanilla
   1 cup whipping cream

Advance Preparation: Slice 1-inch off top of cake; set aside. Cut down into cake; remove interior, leaving 1-inch thick shell. In saucepan combine marshmallows, water, and salt. Cook and stir over low heat till smooth. Add chocolate and vanilla; stir till chocolate melts. Cool. Whip cream till soft peaks form; fold in chocolate mixture. Fill hollowed cake; replace top. Refrigerate up to 24 hours.
Before serving: If desired, frost cake with additional whipped cream or sprinkle with powdered sugar. Makes 12 to 16 servings.

Polynesian Parfaits

Advance preparation: Combine one 8-ounce carton pineapple yogurt, 1 tablespoon sugar, and ⅛ teaspoon ground nutmeg. Drain one 11-ounce can mandarin orange sections and one 8¾-ounce can pineapple tidbits well. In parfait glasses layer yogurt mixture with oranges and pineapple. Refrigerate up to 24 hours. Serves 4.

Chocolate Layer Pie

Advance preparation: Cook one 3¾- or 4-ounce package *regular* chocolate pudding mix according to package directions for pie; cover surface with waxed paper and cool. Prepare one 3⅝- or 3¾-ounce package *instant* vanilla pudding mix according to package directions for pie, *except* use only 1 cup milk and add 1 cup dairy sour cream. Beat *1 cup* of the prepared vanilla pudding into cooled chocolate pudding till smooth. Spread evenly in a *baked* 9-inch pastry shell. Add 2 tablespoons milk to remaining vanilla pudding, beating till smooth. Spread over chocolate filling immediately. Chill till set. Garnish with chocolate curls.

Grasshopper Pie

Advance preparation: For crust line the bottom and sides of a 9-inch pie plate with chocolate wafers.

Combine 6½ cups tiny *marshmallows* and ¼ cup *milk*. Cook, stirring constantly, till marshmallows are melted. Remove from heat. Cool, stirring every 5 minutes. Combine ¼ cup green *crème de menthe* and 2 tablespoons white *crème de cacao*; stir into marshmallow mixture. Whip 2 cups *whipping cream*. Fold marshmallow mixture into whipped cream; turn into crust. Freeze several hours or overnight till firm. Garnish pie with additional unsweetened *whipped cream* and *chocolate curls*.

With a Grasshopper Pie *in the freezer, can a party be far away? Make the pie several days in advance of mid-week or Friday-night entertaining. Garnish with whipped cream and chocolate curls just before serving.*

Broiled Meat Loaf

    3 tablespoons milk
    2 tablespoons fine dry bread crumbs
    2 teaspoons finely chopped green
        onion
    2 teaspoons snipped parsley
    ¼ teaspoon Worcestershire sauce
    ¼ teaspoon salt
        Dash ground nutmeg
    ½ pound ground beef
        Mushroom Sauce

Preheat broiler. In mixing bowl combine milk, fine dry bread crumbs, green onion, parsley, Worcestershire sauce, salt, nutmeg, and dash pepper. Add ground beef; mix well. Pat meat mixture into a square about ¾ inch thick. Cut the square in half to form two rectangles. Broil meat rectangles about 4 inches from heat to desired degree of doneness, turning once. (Allow about 5 minutes on each side for medium.) Serve with Mushroom Sauce. Makes 2 servings.

Mushroom Sauce: Drain *half* of a 3-ounce can sliced mushrooms. In small saucepan melt 1 tablespoon butter. Stir in 1 teaspoon all-purpose flour and dash pepper. Add ¼ cup milk all at once. Cook and stir till thickened and bubbly. Stir in drained mushrooms; heat through.

Chili-Hominy Skillet

    1 pound ground beef
    1 16-ounce can yellow hominy,
        drained
    ¼ cup fresh or frozen chopped
        green pepper
    ¼ cup water
    ½ envelope chili seasoning mix
        (2 tablespoons)
    2 tablespoons onion soup mix
    ½ cup shredded natural Cheddar
        cheese (2 ounces)

Brown the beef; drain off fat. Stir in hominy, green pepper, water, chili seasoning, and soup mix. Cook and stir till heated through, about 5 minutes. Sprinkle cheese over; cover and cook till cheese melts. Serves 4.

Dijon-Style Liver

A delicious liver and onion dish—

    ⅓ cup sliced green onion with tops
    2 tablespoons butter or margarine
    ¼ cup all-purpose flour
    ¼ teaspoon salt
        Dash pepper
    1 pound calf's liver, cut ¾ inch
        thick (4 slices)
    1 tablespoon water
    2 teaspoons Dijon-style mustard
    2 teaspoons Worcestershire sauce
    1 teaspoon lemon juice

In skillet cook green onion in 1 *tablespoon* of the butter till tender but not brown; remove from skillet. Combine flour, salt, and pepper; dip liver in flour mixture to coat. In same skillet melt remaining butter. Cook liver in butter over medium heat for 3 minutes. Turn liver; cook 3 minutes more. Remove to warm platter. Return onion to skillet along with water, mustard, Worcestershire, and lemon juice; cook and stir till heated through. Spoon mustard sauce over liver. Makes 4 servings.

Wine-Sauced Hamburger Steak

    ¾ pound lean ground beef
    ½ teaspoon salt
        Dash pepper

• • •

    1 tablespoon butter or margarine
    2 tablespoons dry red wine
    2 teaspoons dried parsley flakes
    1 teaspoon lemon juice
    ½ teaspoon instant minced onion
    ¼ teaspoon Worcestershire sauce

Combine ground beef, salt, and pepper; mix well. Shape into 2 patties about ½ inch thick. In skillet melt butter. Cook meat to desired doneness, turning once. (Allow 2 minutes on each side for medium-rare.) Remove meat to warm plates. In same skillet combine wine, parsley flakes, lemon juice, instant minced onion, and Worcestershire sauce; heat to boiling. Pour over meat. Makes 2 servings.

Jiffy Steak au Poivre

Flame these at the table —

    2 beef cube steaks
    1 teaspoon freshly ground pepper
    2 tablespoons butter or
        margarine
    Salt
      • • •
    2 tablespoons brandy

Sprinkle beef cube steaks on both sides with freshly ground pepper, pressing in firmly with hands. In medium skillet brown the steaks very quickly in butter or margarine, about 1 minute on each side. Sprinkle with salt. Add brandy to skillet; flame. Remove steaks to warm serving platter; pour pan drippings over. Makes 2 servings.

Stir-Fry Beef with Asparagus

A perfect use for a wok —

    1 pound beef flank steak, partially
        frozen
    2 tablespoons soy sauce
    1 tablespoon cornstarch
    1 tablespoon cooking oil
      • • •
    12 fresh asparagus spears
        Boiling water
    3 tablespoons cooking oil
    1 teaspoon sugar
    2 tablespoons dry sherry
    2 tablespoons chicken broth

Using a sharp knife, cut the flank steak across the grain into very thin slices. Combine soy sauce, cornstarch, and the 1 tablespoon cooking oil; pour over beef slices and stir to coat all meat. Cut fresh asparagus on the bias into 1-inch pieces. Drop asparagus pieces into pan of boiling water. Simmer 1 to 2 minutes. Drain well. Heat the 3 tablespoons cooking oil in skillet or wok till sizzling. Sprinkle sugar over hot oil. Add beef strips; cook and stir quickly for 1 minute. Add asparagus pieces; cook, stirring constantly, 1 minute more. Stir in the dry sherry and the chicken broth; cook ½ minute more. Makes 4 servings.

Planning Menus Saves Time

Spend some time each week planning the week's menus and your shopping list (see page 82). Then, buy all the groceries in one shopping trip. This way, preparation will proceed smoothly because you'll have everything you need on hand.

Barbecue-Sauced Kabobs

Meat and vegetable kabobs shown on page 4 —

    ½ cup hot-style catsup
    2 tablespoons packed brown sugar
    1 tablespoon lemon juice
    1 tablespoon vinegar
    1 teaspoon Worcestershire sauce
    1 medium zucchini, cut in 1-inch
        slices and halved (½ pound)
        Cooking oil
    1 pound beef sirloin, cut in 1½-
        inch cubes
    1 16-ounce can whole white potatoes
        Snipped parsley
        Hot cooked rice

Preheat broiler. Combine first 5 ingredients. Brush zucchini lightly with oil. On 4 long skewers alternately thread beef, potatoes, and zucchini. Brush with catsup mixture. Broil 4 to 5 inches from heat for about 20 minutes; turn once and brush occasionally with sauce. Stir parsley into rice. Serve kabobs on rice. Serves 4.

Curried Shrimp and Peas

    1 10½-ounce can condensed cream of
        celery soup
    ⅔ cup milk
    1 teaspoon curry powder
    2 4½-ounce cans shrimp, drained
    1 8-ounce can peas, drained
        Toast points

In saucepan combine soup, milk, and curry; heat to boiling. Stir in shrimp and peas; heat through. Serve over toast. Serves 4.

Cheesy Tuna

    3 tablespoons butter or margarine
    3 tablespoons all-purpose flour
    ¼ teaspoon salt
    ⅛ teaspoon pepper
    1¾ cups milk
    ½ teaspoon Worcestershire sauce
    ⅓ cup grated Parmesan and Romano
        cheese
    1 6½- or 7-ounce can tuna, drained
    2 tablespoons chopped canned
        pimiento
    Patty shells or toast points

In saucepan melt butter or margarine. Stir in flour, salt, and pepper. Add milk and Worcestershire sauce. Cook over medium heat, stirring constantly, till mixture is thickened and bubbly. Cook and stir 1 minute more. Stir in grated cheese. Cook over low heat till cheese melts, about 1 minute. Stir in tuna and pimiento; heat through. Spoon mixture into baked patty shells or over toast points. Makes 6 servings.

Macaroni-Salmon Skillet

A fix-up for macaroni and cheese mix—

    1 7¼- or 8-ounce package macaroni
        and cheese dinner mix
    ¾ cup milk
    2 tablespoons butter or margarine
    1 16-ounce can salmon, drained and
        broken into chunks
    1 3-ounce can sliced mushrooms
    2 teaspoons dried parsley flakes
    ½ teaspoon paprika
    ½ teaspoon prepared mustard
    1 cup dairy sour cream
    2 tablespoons dry white wine

Cook macaroni from dinner mix according to package directions; drain. In skillet combine cooked macaroni, the cheese from dinner mix, milk, and butter or margarine. Stir in salmon, undrained mushrooms, parsley, paprika, and mustard. Simmer, uncovered, for 5 to 10 minutes, stirring occasionally. Stir in sour cream and wine; heat through. Makes 4 or 5 servings.

Scallop Fondue

    1 12-ounce package frozen scallops,
        thawed
    1 beaten egg
    ¼ cup milk
    ⅔ cup fine dry bread crumbs
        Cooking oil
        Dill Sauce or Zippy Sauce

Halve large scallops. Rinse and drain scallops; pat dry with paper toweling. Mix egg and milk. Mix crumbs, ½ teaspoon salt, and dash pepper. Dip scallops into egg mixture; roll in crumbs. Shake off excess crumbs. Pour oil into metal fondue cooker to no more than ½ capacity or to depth of 2 inches. Heat over range to 375°. Add 1 teaspoon salt. Transfer cooker to fondue burner. Spear scallops with fondue fork; fry in hot oil till browned. Dip in Dill Sauce or Zippy Sauce. Serves 2 or 3.

Dill Sauce: Mix one 8-ounce container sour cream dip with chives, 2 tablespoons milk, 1 teaspoon lemon juice, and ½ teaspoon dried dillweed. Makes 1 cup.

Zippy Sauce: Combine ½ cup chili sauce, 1 tablespoon lemon juice, 1 teaspoon prepared horseradish, 1 teaspoon Worcestershire sauce, and dash bottled hot pepper sauce; mix well. Makes ½ cup.

Herbed Halibut Sauterne

    2 fresh or frozen halibut steaks
    1 tablespoon fresh or frozen chopped
        onion
    2 tablespoons butter or margarine
    ¼ cup sauterne
    2 teaspoons lemon juice
    ½ teaspoon dried parsley flakes
    ⅛ teaspoon dried rosemary, crushed

Thaw frozen fish. Preheat broiler. Cook onion in butter till tender. Add next 4 ingredients. Simmer 3 to 4 minutes. Sprinkle fish with salt; brush with wine mixture. Broil 5 to 6 inches from heat for 16 minutes; turn once and brush occasionally with wine mixture. Heat remaining wine mixture; serve over fish. Serves 2.

Saucy Poached Fish

　¼ cup dry sherry
　1 10¾-ounce can condensed cream of
　　　mushroom soup
　¼ teaspoon dry mustard
　4 fresh or frozen halibut steaks
　1 3-ounce can sliced mushrooms
　2 tablespoons snipped parsley
　　Hot cooked rice

In medium skillet gradually stir sherry into soup. Stir in mustard. Bring to boil; reduce heat. Separate frozen fish; place fish in hot soup mixture. Cook, covered, till fish flakes easily, about 10 minutes. Carefully remove fish to warm platter. Drain mushrooms; stir mushrooms and parsley into soup mixture. Heat through; serve over fish and hot cooked rice. Makes 4 servings.

Lazy-Day Lobster Newburg

　1⅓ cups light cream
　1 envelope white sauce mix
　　　(enough for 1 cup sauce)
　2 beaten egg yolks
　1 5-ounce can lobster, drained,
　　　flaked, and cartilage removed
　2 tablespoons dry sherry
　　Patty shells or toast points
　　Paprika

Gradually blend cream into sauce mix; cook and stir till thickened and bubbly. Stir small amount hot liquid into yolks; return to hot mixture. Cook and stir till bubbly. Stir in lobster and sherry; heat through. Serve in baked patty shells or over toast; sprinkle with paprika. Serves 4.

Bean-Sausage Combo

In saucepan combine one 16- or 18-ounce can baked beans; one 16-ounce can cut green beans, drained; one 8½-ounce can lima beans; and 2 teaspoons instant minced onion. Stir in one 12-ounce package smoked sausage links, bias-cut in pieces. Heat through, stirring occasionally. Serves 4.

Chinese Pork and Vegetables

　¼ cup soy sauce
　1 tablespoon cornstarch
　2 tablespoons cooking oil
　1 clove garlic, minced
　1 teaspoon grated gingerroot
　1 pound lean pork, diced
　3 cups chopped Chinese or celery
　　　cabbage
　1 10-ounce package frozen peas,
　　　thawed
　1 medium green pepper, cut in
　　　thin strips
　1 3-ounce can sliced mushrooms,
　　　drained
　2 tablespoons sliced green onion
　2 tablespoons dry sherry
　　Hot cooked rice

Combine soy sauce, cornstarch, and ½ cup water; set aside. Heat oil in wok or electric skillet. Add garlic, gingerroot, and dash salt; stir-fry at medium heat just till garlic is golden. Turn heat to high; add pork gradually. Stir constantly till browned, 2 to 4 minutes. Season with salt. Add cabbage, peas, green pepper, mushrooms, green onion, and sherry. Cook and stir 1 minute more. Pour soy mixture over vegetables; cook and stir till thickened. Serve over rice. Serves 4 or 5.

Quick Pork Curry

　1 tomato, peeled and chopped
　¼ cup fresh or frozen chopped onion
　1 to 2 teaspoons curry powder
　1 tablespoon butter or margarine
　1 10½-ounce can condensed golden
　　　mushroom soup
　½ cup milk
　1½ to 2 cups cubed cooked pork
　1 cup dairy sour cream
　　Hot cooked rice

Cook tomato, onion, curry, and ¼ teaspoon salt in butter till onion is tender. Stir in soup and milk. Add pork; simmer 10 minutes. Stir in sour cream; heat through, but *do not boil.* Serve over rice. Serves 4 or 5.

Cheese soup and caraway seed add a new twist to the popular combination of frankfurters and sauerkraut in Frank-Kraut Dinner. For a special touch, slash the frankfurters before placing them atop the sauerkraut.

Frank-Kraut Dinner

¼ cup milk
1 11-ounce can condensed Cheddar
   cheese soup
½ teaspoon caraway seed
½ teaspoon prepared mustard
1 27-ounce can sauerkraut, drained
1 pound frankfurters (8 to 10)

Preheat oven to 375°. Gradually stir milk into soup till blended; stir in caraway and mustard. Snip sauerkraut; fold into soup mixture. Heat through, stirring often. Turn into 10x6x1½-inch baking dish. Slash frankfurters diagonally at 1-inch intervals; arrange atop casserole. Bake at 375° for 15 to 20 minutes. Makes 4 servings.

Frank-Egg Scramble

4 or 5 frankfurters
1 tablespoon sugar
1 tablespoon soy sauce
½ medium onion, sliced and separated
   into rings
½ medium green pepper, cut in ¼-
   inch-wide strips
6 beaten eggs

Slice franks diagonally into ½-inch-wide pieces. In skillet brown the franks. Remove from heat; push to one side. Stir in sugar and soy. Add vegetables. Cook, covered, till vegetables are crisp-tender, about 3 minutes. Pour eggs over. Cook and stir till eggs are set. Makes 4 to 6 servings.

Bacon-Bean Skillet

2 16-ounce cans pork and beans in
   tomato sauce
3 spiced peaches, coarsely chopped
¼ cup catsup
2 tablespoons packed brown sugar
2 teaspoons instant minced onion
2 teaspoons prepared mustard
2 teaspoons Worcestershire sauce
8 slices Canadian-style bacon

In 10-inch skillet combine first 7 ingredients. Cook, uncovered, over medium heat till thick, about 8 minutes, stirring often. Place bacon atop. Cover; cook till bacon is hot, about 4 minutes. Makes 4 servings.

Ham Barbecue

1 cup cubed fully cooked ham
1 teaspoon cooking oil
1 8¾-ounce can pineapple tidbits
¼ cup bottled barbecue sauce
⅓ cup cold water
1½ teaspoons cornstarch
½ medium green pepper, cut in strips
   Hot cooked rice

Brown the meat lightly in hot oil in skillet. Drain pineapple, reserving syrup. Stir reserved syrup and barbecue sauce into browned meat. Cover; simmer 10 minutes. Blend cold water and cornstarch; stir into meat mixture. Cook and stir till thickened and bubbly. Add pineapple and green pepper. Heat through. Serve over rice. Serves 2.

Microwave Cooking

Microwave ovens are one of the newest timesaving kitchen appliances. They are suited particularly for cooking small quantities of food quickly and for cutting to seconds or minutes the time needed to reheat or defrost foods. Be sure to follow the manufacturer's instructions accompanying your microwave oven.

Apricot-Glazed Ham

1 8¾-ounce can unpeeled apricot
   halves
2 tablespoons packed brown sugar
2 teaspoons vinegar
1 teaspoon prepared mustard
¼ teaspoon ground ginger
1 1½-pound fully cooked ham slice
6 maraschino cherries

Drain apricots, reserving 2 tablespoons syrup. Set aside 6 apricot halves; press remaining apricots through sieve. Combine sieved apricots, reserved syrup, brown sugar, vinegar, mustard, and ginger. Trim excess fat from ham; slash remaining fat edges. In skillet cook trimmings till 1 tablespoon fat accumulates. Discard trimmings. Brown the ham slowly on one side in hot fat, about 4 minutes; turn. Place reserved apricot halves atop; spoon apricot mixture over. Cover; cook 5 minutes. Garnish each apricot half with cherry. Serves 6.

Ham Grab Bags

1 16-ounce can sweet potatoes
1 16-ounce package ham steaks
   (8 slices)
1 16-ounce can Italian green beans,
   drained
1 20-ounce can pie-sliced apples,
   drained
1 8-ounce can whole cranberry sauce
½ teaspoon Dijon-style mustard
¼ cup packed brown sugar (optional)

Preheat oven to 400°. Drain sweet potatoes, reserving 1 tablespoon syrup; slice sweet potatoes. On four sheets of heavy foil, layer the ham slices, sweet potatoes, beans, and apples. Combine cranberry sauce, reserved sweet potato syrup, and mustard. Spoon cranberry mixture over ham and vegetables. If desired, sprinkle apple slices and sweet potatoes with brown sugar. Wrap up foil pouches loosely. Place on baking sheet. Bake at 400° till heated through, about 20 minutes. Transfer to serving plates, pouring juices over all. Makes 4 servings.

Ham with Spicy Raisin Sauce

    1 1½-pound fully cooked ham slice,
        cut 1 inch thick
    ½ cup packed brown sugar
    ½ teaspoon dry mustard
    ¼ teaspoon ground ginger
    1 22-ounce can raisin pie filling
    2 tablespoons vinegar
    2 tablespoons water
    ½ teaspoon Worcestershire sauce

Preheat broiler. Slash fat edge of ham. Broil about 3 inches from heat for 14 to 16 minutes, turning once. Meanwhile, in saucepan blend together brown sugar, dry mustard, and ginger. Stir in raisin pie filling, vinegar, water, and Worcestershire sauce; heat to boiling. Serve raisin sauce with ham. Makes 6 servings.

Meat and Rice Skillet

    ½ cup fresh or frozen chopped onion
    ½ cup fresh or frozen chopped green
        pepper
    2 tablespoons cooking oil
            • • •
    1 29-ounce can tomatoes, cut up
    1 12-ounce can luncheon meat, cut
        in cubes
    1¾ cups water
    1 teaspoon paprika
    1 bay leaf
    ½ teaspoon dried thyme, crushed
    ½ teaspoon dried oregano, crushed
    ¼ teaspoon garlic powder
    3 drops bottled hot pepper sauce
        Dash pepper
    1½ cups uncooked packaged precooked
        rice

In large skillet cook onion and green pepper in hot oil till tender. Stir in tomatoes, cubed luncheon meat, water, paprika, bay leaf, thyme, oregano, garlic powder, bottled hot pepper sauce, and pepper. Cover; simmer 15 minutes. Stir in rice. Cover; simmer 2 minutes more. Remove pan from heat; let stand, covered, for 5 minutes. Remove bay leaf before serving. Makes 6 servings.

Speedy Chicken Chasseur

Pick up the fried chicken for this dish on your way home from work—

    2 medium tomatoes, peeled and
        chopped
    1 3-ounce can sliced mushrooms,
        drained
    ⅔ cup dry white wine
    2 tablespoons butter or margarine
    2 chicken bouillon cubes
    1 tablespoon instant minced onion
    1 tablespoon lemon juice
    1 teaspoon sugar
    ¼ teaspoon salt
    ⅛ teaspoon dried oregano, crushed
    2 teaspoons cornstarch
    8 carry-out fried chicken legs

In 10-inch skillet combine chopped tomatoes, mushrooms, *half* the wine, butter or margarine, bouillon, instant minced onion, lemon juice, sugar, salt, and oregano. Bring to a boil; cover and simmer till tomatoes are tender, about 3 minutes. Blend together cornstarch and remaining wine; stir into mixture. Cook, stirring constantly, till thickened and bubbly. Add carry-out fried chicken; simmer till heated through, about 5 minutes. Makes 4 servings.

Turkey Gumbo

A delicious use for leftover turkey—

    1 cup water
    2 tablespoons cornstarch
    1 tablespoon soy sauce
    1 10½-ounce can condensed chicken
        gumbo soup
    2 cups cubed cooked turkey
    2 tablespoons chopped canned
        pimiento
    1 3-ounce can chow mein noodles
        (2¼ cups)

In saucepan combine water, cornstarch, and soy sauce. Stir in chicken gumbo soup. Cook, stirring constantly, till thickened and bubbly. Stir in cubed turkey and chopped pimiento. Heat through. Serve over chow mein noodles. Makes 4 servings.

Oriental Chicken

An especially colorful dish—

>2 cups cubed cooked chicken
>2 cups chicken broth
>1 6-ounce package frozen pea pods
>1 5-ounce can water chestnuts,
>>drained and thinly sliced
>
>2 tablespoons sliced green onion
>½ teaspoon ground ginger
>¼ cup cornstarch
>¼ cup cold water
>3 tablespoons soy sauce
>2 medium tomatoes, cut in wedges
>
>• • •
>
>Chow mein noodles, warmed, or
>hot cooked rice

In skillet or wok combine chicken, chicken broth, pea pods, water chestnuts, green onion, and ginger; heat to boiling. Combine cornstarch, water, and soy sauce; stir into chicken mixture. Cook and stir till mixture is thickened and bubbly. Add tomato wedges and heat just till hot. Serve on chow mein noodles or cooked rice. Pass additional soy sauce, if desired. Serves 4 or 5.

"Ole!" is what they'll say after sampling this Mexi-Chicken Skillet. *Canned chili peppers and tamales in it account for its south-of-the-border name.*

Creamed Turkey Especial

>1½ teaspoons instant chicken
>>bouillon granules
>
>1 cup boiling water
>1 cup light cream
>2 packages white sauce mix (each
>>enough for 1 cup sauce)
>
>1½ cups cubed cooked turkey
>1 8-ounce can water chestnuts,
>>drained and sliced
>
>¼ cup dry sherry
>2 tablespoons finely snipped parsley
>3 English muffins, split and toasted
>Paprika

Dissolve bouillon in boiling water. Add cream. Prepare sauce mix according to package directions, *except* use cream mixture in place of liquid called for. Stir in turkey, water chestnuts, sherry, and parsley; heat through. Spoon over English muffin halves. Sprinkle with paprika. Makes 6 servings.

Mexi-Chicken Skillet

In skillet combine 2 cups cubed cooked chicken; one 11-ounce can condensed Cheddar cheese soup; one 8-ounce can tomatoes, cut up; ½ cup uncooked packaged precooked rice; and 2 tablespoons chopped canned green chili peppers. Drain sauce from one 15-ounce can tamales and add sauce to chicken mixture. Cover; simmer 5 minutes over low heat. Meanwhile, remove husks from tamales; cut tamales in 1-inch pieces. Place pieces atop chicken mixture. Cover; cook over low heat till tamales are heated through, about 10 minutes. Serves 4.

Chicken Shortcake

Use canned or leftover cooked chicken—

 1 package refrigerated buttermilk
    biscuits (10 biscuits)
    Butter or margarine, melted
 1 10¾-ounce can condensed cream
    of mushroom soup
 1 10½-ounce can condensed cream
    chicken soup
 ¼ cup milk
 2 cups cubed cooked chicken
 1 3-ounce can sliced mushrooms,
    drained
 ¼ cup chopped green onion
 1 tablespoon chopped canned pimiento

Preheat oven to 475°. Remove refrigerated biscuits from package. Flatten biscuits with hand to make circles about 3 inches in diameter. Place 5 biscuits on baking sheet; brush with a little melted butter or margarine. Top each biscuit with another biscuit. Press edges together. Bake at 475° till browned, 7 to 8 minutes. Meanwhile, in large saucepan blend mushroom soup, chicken soup, and milk. Add cubed chicken, mushrooms, green onion, and pimiento. Cook over low heat, stirring occasionally, till heated through. To serve, separate double biscuits; place bottom half on plate. Pour on some chicken sauce; add top biscuit and pour more sauce over. Serves 5.

Chicken Livers Stroganoff

An unusual dish for two—

 1 cup thinly sliced onion
 2 tablespoons butter or margarine
 4 ounces chicken livers, halved
 1½ teaspoons paprika
 ½ cup dairy sour cream
    Hot cooked noodles

Cook onion in butter till tender. Add chicken livers. Season with paprika, ¼ teaspoon salt, and dash pepper. Slowly brown the livers. Cover and cook over low heat till livers are tender, about 10 minutes. Add sour cream; heat through, but *do not boil.* Serve over noodles. Makes 2 servings.

Chicken Dinner Omelet

Crouton-filled omelet shown on page 32—

 1 10½-ounce can chicken à la king
 2 tablespoons chopped canned
    pimiento
 ¼ cup fresh or frozen chopped onion
 ¼ cup chopped celery
 3 tablespoons butter or margarine
 ½ cup garlic croutons
 5 slightly beaten eggs
 ½ cup milk
 ½ teaspoon salt

Combine chicken à la king and pimiento; heat through. Meanwhile, in 10-inch skillet cook onion and celery in butter till tender. Add croutons; toss lightly. Remove mixture from skillet. Combine eggs, milk, and salt; pour into hot skillet. Cook slowly, lifting eggs to allow uncooked portion to flow under. Place vegetable-crouton mixture on half the omelet; fold over. Tilt pan and roll omelet onto hot plate. Pour chicken mixture over. Makes 2 or 3 servings.

Sausage and Hashed Brown Omelet

 ½ pound bulk pork sausage
 2 cups shredded cooked potato
    (2 medium potatoes)
 ¼ cup fresh or frozen chopped onion
 ¼ cup fresh or frozen chopped green
    pepper
 4 eggs
 ¼ cup milk
 ½ cup shredded process American
    cheese (2 ounces)

In large skillet brown the sausage. Drain sausage, reserving ¼ cup drippings; set sausage aside. Return reserved drippings to skillet. Combine potato, onion, and green pepper; pat into skillet. Season generously with salt; sprinkle with pepper. Cook over low heat till underside is crisp and brown. Blend eggs, milk, ¼ teaspoon salt, and dash pepper. Pour over potatoes. Top with cheese and sausage. Cover; cook over low heat for 6 to 8 minutes. Loosen omelet; cut in wedges to serve. Makes 4 servings.

Count on canned vegetables, soup, and meatballs to help you put Confetti Meatball Supper together in a hurry. For extra eye appeal, shape the rice in a ring mold and spoon the meatballs with gravy in the center.

Confetti Meatball Supper

Keep canned meatballs on hand for this dish—

In skillet combine one 11-ounce can condensed Cheddar cheese soup, ¼ cup catsup, 1 teaspoon instant minced onion, and 1 teaspoon Worcestershire sauce. Heat through. Add two 15-ounce cans meatballs in gravy; simmer till heated through.

Meanwhile, in saucepan combine 2 cups uncooked packaged precooked rice; 2 cups water; one 8½-ounce can mixed vegetables, drained; 2 tablespoons chopped canned pimiento; and ¼ teaspoon salt. Bring to boiling. Cover. Remove from heat; let stand 5 minutes. Press rice mixture lightly into oiled 4½-cup ring mold. Unmold at once onto hot platter. Fill center of rice ring with meatballs and some of the sauce. Pass remaining sauce. Makes 4 to 6 servings.

Indian Pizza

An unusual fix-up for frozen pizza—

   ½ cup fresh or frozen chopped green
      pepper
   ½ cup fresh or frozen chopped onion
   1 tablespoon cooking oil
   2 12-inch frozen cheese pizzas
      Curry powder
   1 cup chopped cooked chicken
   1 cup shredded natural mozzarella
      cheese (4 ounces)

Preheat oven. Cook green pepper and onion in oil till tender. Sprinkle each pizza generously with curry powder. Arrange green pepper, onion, cooked chicken, and mozzarella over each pizza. Sprinkle curry powder over top. Bake according to package directions. Makes 4 to 6 servings.

Corn Rarebit

½ cup fresh or frozen chopped green
   pepper
2 tablespoons fresh or frozen
   chopped onion
2 tablespoons butter or margarine
1 tablespoon all-purpose flour
¼ teaspoon chili powder
1 cup tomato juice
1 8-ounce can whole kernel corn,
   drained
1 cup shredded process American
   cheese (4 ounces)
½ cup sliced pitted ripe olives
   English muffins, split and toasted

In saucepan cook green pepper and onion
in butter till tender but not brown. Blend in
flour and chili powder. Stir in tomato juice
and corn, blending well. Cook, stirring constantly, till thickened. Stir in shredded
cheese and olives; cook and stir over low
heat till cheese melts. Serve over English
muffins. Makes 4 servings.

Speedy Italian Cheese Fondue

1 15½-ounce can meatless spaghetti
   sauce
⅓ cup dry red wine
3 cups shredded process American
   cheese (12 ounces)
1 cup shredded natural mozzarella
   cheese (4 ounces)
2 teaspoons cornstarch
   Italian bread, cut in bite-size
   pieces, each with one crust

In saucepan combine spaghetti sauce and
wine; cook over *low* heat just till mixture
bubbles. Add American cheese gradually,
stirring till melted. Coat mozzarella cheese
with cornstarch; add gradually to fondue
mixture. Continue to cook and stir over low
heat till cheese is melted. Transfer to fondue pot. Place over fondue burner. Spear
bread cube with fondue fork; dip in fondue
mixture, swirling to coat. (If fondue becomes thick, stir in a little *warmed* wine.)
Makes 6 servings.

Guacamole Burgers

Topped with a tasty avocado-tomato mixture —

1 pound ground beef
½ cup crushed corn chips
⅓ cup milk
1 teaspoon Worcestershire sauce
½ teaspoon onion salt
     • • •
1 7¾-ounce can frozen avocado dip,
   thawed
1 tablespoon lemon juice
   Few drops bottled hot pepper sauce
1 small tomato, peeled and chopped
5 hamburger buns, split and toasted

Preheat broiler. Mix together ground beef,
crushed corn chips, milk, Worcestershire
sauce, and onion salt. Shape into 5 patties.
Broil beef patties 3 inches from heat for 6
minutes; turn and broil till done, about 4
minutes more. Meanwhile, combine avocado dip, lemon juice, and hot pepper
sauce. Stir in chopped tomato. Place hamburgers on bottom halves of toasted buns;
top with avocado mixture. Replace bun
tops. Makes 5 sandwiches.

Creamy Beefburgers

Dairy sour cream adds flavor —

1 pound ground beef
¼ cup fresh or frozen chopped onion
1 tablespoon all-purpose flour
¼ teaspoon salt
1 10¾-ounce can condensed vegetable
   soup
½ teaspoon Worcestershire sauce
1 cup dairy sour cream
8 hamburger buns, split and toasted

In skillet cook ground beef and chopped
onion till beef is browned and onion is
tender; drain off excess fat. Blend flour
and salt into beef mixture; add vegetable
soup and Worcestershire sauce. Cook, stirring constantly, till mixture is bubbly. Stir
in dairy sour cream; heat 1 minute more
(do not boil). Spoon beef mixture onto
bottom halves of toasted buns; replace
tops. Makes 8 sandwiches.

Barbecued Frank Sandwiches

¼ cup fresh or frozen chopped onion
1 tablespoon butter or margarine
4 or 5 frankfurters, thinly sliced
1 cup applesauce
½ cup hot-style catsup
2 tablespoons vinegar
1 tablespoon packed brown sugar
4 or 5 French rolls, split lengthwise, toasted, and buttered

Cook onion in butter till tender. Add next 5 ingredients and ½ teaspoon salt. Simmer, uncovered, 15 to 20 minutes. Serve in French rolls. Makes 4 or 5 sandwiches.

Ham-Avocado Sandwiches

1 tablespoon lemon juice
1 teaspoon prepared horseradish
   Dash bottled hot pepper sauce
⅓ cup mayonnaise or salad dressing
1 medium avocado, peeled and pitted
10 slices rye sandwich bread
5 slices natural Swiss cheese
10 slices boiled ham
1 medium tomato, sliced
   Lettuce

Combine first 3 ingredients and ¼ teaspoon salt. Fold in mayonnaise. Slice avocado. Atop *each* of 5 slices bread place cheese slice, 2 rolled ham slices, avocado, tomato, and lettuce. Drizzle with mayonnaise mixture. Cover with remaining bread. Makes 5.

Corned Beef Hash Burgers

Preheat broiler. Split and toast 8 onion rolls. Mix one 15-ounce can corned beef hash, ⅓ cup dairy sour cream, 1 tablespoon sweet pickle relish, and 1 teaspoon prepared horseradish. Spread about ¼ cup on bottom half of each roll. Broil 3 to 4 inches from heat till heated through, about 5 minutes. Top *each* sandwich with a slice of tomato and a slice of process American cheese; broil just till cheese melts. Cover with tops of rolls. Makes 8.

Liver Sausage Special
Delicious served cold or grilled—

8 slices Russian rye bread
   Bottled mustard sauce
8 slices smoked liver sausage
   (4 to 5 ounces)
4 slices process Swiss cheese,
   halved lengthwise (4 ounces)
4 green pepper rings
1 8-ounce can sauerkraut, rinsed
   and drained
   Snipped parsley
   Butter or margarine, melted
   (optional)

Spread bread with mustard sauce. On *each* of 4 slices bread, place 2 slices liver sausage, 2 pieces cheese, 1 green pepper ring, *one-fourth* of the sauerkraut, and some parsley. Top with remaining bread. Serve cold or brush with butter and grill on both sides. Makes 4 sandwiches.

Puffy Sandwich Omelet
Use beaten egg white for a puffy topping—

1 egg
2 egg yolks
2 slices bacon, crisp-cooked,
   drained, and crumbled
1 tablespoon light cream
2 teaspoons butter or margarine
2 slices white bread, toasted and
   buttered
2 stiffly beaten egg whites

Preheat oven to 350°. In medium bowl beat together the whole egg, egg yolks, bacon, light cream, dash salt, and dash pepper with a fork till just combined. In small skillet melt butter or margarine. Add egg mixture to the melted butter and cook quickly till egg is set but still glossy. Fold cooked eggs in half; cut into 2 pieces. On baking sheet place *each half* egg mixture on a buttered slice of toast. Cover both sandwiches entirely with stiffly beaten egg whites. Sprinkle with salt and pepper. Bake at 350° just till egg whites are golden, about 10 minutes. Makes 2 sandwiches.

Jiffy Barbecue Boats

½ cup fresh or frozen chopped onion
½ cup sliced celery
2 tablespoons butter or margarine
1 cup catsup
¼ cup packed brown sugar
3 tablespoons vinegar
1 tablespoon prepared mustard
1 tablespoon Worcestershire sauce
1 12-ounce can luncheon meat, cut
   in strips
6 frankfurter buns, split and
   toasted

In skillet cook onion and celery in butter till tender. Stir in catsup, brown sugar, vinegar, mustard, Worcestershire, and ⅓ cup water. Stir in meat. Simmer, uncovered, till heated through, about 15 minutes. Spoon into buns. Makes 6 servings.

A-B-C Club Sandwiches

⅓ cup mayonnaise or salad dressing
2 tablespoons dairy sour cream
1 tablespoon lemon juice
8 slices bacon, crisp-cooked,
   drained, and crumbled
¼ cup finely chopped celery
¼ cup finely chopped radish
1 7½-ounce can crab meat, drained,
   flaked, and cartilage removed
1 medium avocado, seeded, peeled,
   and finely chopped or mashed
¼ teaspoon salt
5 lettuce leaves
15 slices white bread,
   toasted

Combine mayonnaise or salad dressing, sour cream, and lemon juice. Stir bacon, celery, and radish into *half* the mayonnaise mixture. Combine crab, avocado, salt, and remaining mayonnaise mixture. Place lettuce leaves on 5 slices toast. Top *each* with some bacon mixture, then another slice toast. Spread on some crab mixture and top with another slice toast. Secure each sandwich with wooden picks; cut into triangles. Makes 5 sandwiches.

Peanut Butter Wiches

A tasty variation of the all-time favorite, peanut butter and jelly sandwich —

½ cup chunk-style peanut butter
1 small carrot, shredded (¼ cup)
2 tablespoons orange marmalade
8 slices raisin or whole wheat bread

Combine peanut butter, shredded carrot, and orange marmalade. Spread peanut butter mixture on 4 slices bread. Top with remaining bread. Makes 4 sandwiches.

Taco Burgers

1 pound ground beef
1 16-ounce can tomatoes, cut up
1 envelope taco seasoning mix
6 hamburger buns, split and toasted
1 cup shredded natural Cheddar
   cheese (4 ounces)
2 cups shredded lettuce

Brown the beef till crumbly; drain off fat. Add tomatoes and taco seasoning mix. Stir well. Bring to boiling; reduce heat and simmer 10 minutes. Spoon beef mixture over bottom halves of buns. Sprinkle with shredded cheese and lettuce. Cover with tops of buns. Makes 6 sandwiches.

Deviled Ham Sandwiches

A lunch box treat —

4 slices rye bread
   Butter or margarine, softened
1 3-ounce can deviled ham
2 tablespoons sweet pickle relish
1 teaspoon prepared mustard
¼ teaspoon prepared horseradish
   Lettuce

Spread bread with butter. Combine deviled ham, pickle relish, mustard, and horseradish. Spread deviled ham mixture on 2 slices bread. Top with lettuce. (For lunch boxes, pack lettuce and sandwiches separately. Add lettuce when ready to eat.) Top with remaining bread. Makes 2 sandwiches.

Tuna-Tomato Cups

An excellent choice for hot weather menus—

1 6½- or 7-ounce can tuna, drained
    and flaked
½ cup chopped celery
⅓ cup chopped green pepper
2 tablespoons chopped onion
½ to 1 teaspoon curry powder
½ cup mayonnaise or salad dressing

• • •

6 tomatoes
    Lettuce cups

Lightly toss together tuna, celery, green pepper, onion, curry, ¼ teaspoon salt, and dash pepper. Gently stir in mayonnaise. With stem end down, cut each tomato into 6 wedges, *cutting to, but not through,* base of tomato. Spread wedges apart slightly. Sprinkle tomatoes lightly with salt. Fill each tomato with tuna mixture. Place in lettuce cups on platter. Makes 6 servings.

Antipasto Salad

2 cups torn lettuce
1 slice process Swiss cheese, cut
    in strips
4 slices pepperoni (1½ inch diameter)
3 thin slices cooked roast beef,
    cut in strips
1 thin slice fully cooked ham, cut
    in strips
2 tablespoons chopped sweet pickled
    peppers
3 tablespoons salad oil
1 tablespoon wine vinegar
¼ teaspoon garlic salt
¼ teaspoon dried oregano, crushed
1 tablespoon grated Parmesan cheese

Combine first 6 ingredients. In screw-top jar combine oil, vinegar, garlic salt, oregano, ¼ teaspoon salt, and dash pepper; shake well. Pour over salad. Sprinkle with Parmesan; toss. Serves 1 or 2.

Turn plump, garden-fresh tomatoes into colorful, edible salad bowls for Tuna-Tomato Cups. The tuna filling, delicately flavored with curry, also contains crunchy bits of chopped celery, green pepper, and onion.

Side Dishes and Desserts

Cheesy Bean Dip

1 teaspoon instant minced onion
⅓ cup milk
1 15½-ounce can refried beans
1 cup shredded sharp process
    American cheese (4 ounces)
1 tablespoon finely chopped canned
    green chili peppers
    Tortilla chips

In saucepan soften onion in milk. Add beans, cheese, and peppers. Cook and stir till heated through. Pour into small chafing dish. Keep warm over candle or chafing-dish burner. (Thin with more milk, if necessary.) Serve with chips. Makes 2 cups.

Cocktail Reubens

36 slices party rye bread
    Thousand island dressing
1 4-ounce package thinly sliced
    corned beef
1 8-ounce can sauerkraut, drained
    and snipped
6 slices process Swiss cheese

Preheat oven to 400°. Spread bread with dressing. Top with beef; cover with sauerkraut. Cut each slice cheese into 6 pieces; place atop appetizers. Bake on baking sheet at 400° till heated through and cheese melts, 6 to 8 minutes. Makes 36.

Garnishing Hints

Perk up any dish by adding a garnish. Use these simple garnishes for main dishes—sliced tomato, olives, or green pepper, cheese triangles, or paprika. Garnish desserts with cookie decorations, whipped cream, or chocolate curls.

Yogurt-Dressed Salad

1 cucumber, peeled and seeded
1 green pepper, seeded and cut up
3 green onions, cut up
1 8-ounce carton plain yogurt (1 cup)
1 tablespoon salad oil
2 teaspoons seasoned salt
2 teaspoons lemon juice
1 clove garlic, minced
1 head Boston lettuce
1 bunch watercress
1 cup garlic croutons

Cut up cucumber. Place *half* cucumber, *half* green pepper, and *half* onions in blender container; cover and blend till finely chopped. Pour into mixing bowl. Repeat with remaining cucumber, green pepper, and onions. Stir in yogurt, oil, seasoned salt, lemon juice, and garlic. Tear lettuce and watercress into bite-size pieces; combine with croutons in salad bowl. Toss lightly with enough yogurt mixture to coat. Serves 8.

Curried Pear and Cheese Salad

1 29-ounce can pear halves, chilled
    Lettuce
1½ cups cream-style cottage cheese
¼ cup chopped peanuts
¼ cup raisins
½ teaspoon curry powder

Drain pears; slice lengthwise into quarters. Arrange on 6 lettuce-lined plates. Mix remaining ingredients. Mound cheese mixture onto pear slices. Makes 6 servings.

Jiffy accompaniments

Perk up meals with Zucchini with Walnuts (see recipe, page 53), Toasted Bun Sticks (see recipe, page 54), and Pink Cream Dessert (see recipe, page 57). →

Herb Mayonnaise

1 cup mayonnaise or salad dressing
2 tablespoons finely chopped onion
1 clove garlic, minced
1 tablespoon lemon juice
1 tablespoon dry sherry
1 teaspoon Worcestershire sauce
½ teaspoon dried mixed salad herbs

Combine mayonnaise, onion, garlic, lemon juice, sherry, Worcestershire, and herbs; mix well. Makes 1¼ cups.

Chili Mayonnaise

Mix 1 cup mayonnaise or salad dressing and ½ cup chili sauce. Makes 1½ cups.

Pink Fruit Dressing

1 cup mayonnaise or salad dressing
⅓ cup cranberry juice cocktail
   Dash salt
2 tablespoons chopped
   almonds, toasted

Mix mayonnaise or salad dressing, cranberry juice cocktail, and dash salt. Stir in almonds. Makes 1⅓ cups.

Lima Salad

2 hard-cooked eggs
1 16-ounce can lima beans, chilled
   and drained
½ cup diced celery
2 tablespoons sweet pickle relish
⅓ cup mayonnaise or salad dressing
2 tablespoons snipped parsley
2 teaspoons prepared mustard
   Dash bottled hot pepper sauce
   Lettuce cups

Chop one egg. Combine chopped egg, beans, celery, and relish. Blend in mayonnaise, parsley, mustard, hot pepper sauce, and dash salt. Serve in lettuce. Slice remaining egg; use for garnish. Serves 6.

Cran-Appledorf

1 16-ounce can jellied cranberry
   sauce, chilled
¼ cup dairy sour cream
¼ cup frozen whipped dessert
   topping, thawed
2 cups chopped apple
1 cup sliced celery
½ cup chopped walnuts
   Lettuce

Cut jellied cranberry sauce in half; cut half into ¼-inch cubes and set aside. Mash remaining cranberry sauce with fork; fold in sour cream, then whipped topping. Stir in apple, celery, and walnuts. Serve on lettuce-lined plates. Garnish with the cranberry sauce cubes. Makes 6 servings.

Quick Salad Ideas

Add flavor and color to menus by creating an appetizing, quick-to-fix salad. Use the following suggestions as a guide:

● Top a pear half with shredded American or Cheddar cheese.

● Serve slices of tomato and sweet onion with your favorite salad dressing.

● Enhance tossed salads by adding chopped hard-cooked egg; mandarin oranges; raw vegetables such as cauliflower; sliced olives; crumbled bacon or bacon-flavored protein bits; shredded cheese or cheese cubes; leftover cooked vegetables; and/or croutons.

● Fix up bottled salad dressings by mixing them with sour cream or mayonnaise.

● Mix equal amounts of whipped cream and sweet French dressing. Serve with fresh or canned fruit.

● Mound cottage cheese with chives atop tomato halves or slices.

● Serve canned peach or pear halves or pineapple slices with cottage cheese.

● Instead of a salad, serve a relish tray including a variety of raw vegetables, spiced peaches, spiced apple rings, spiced crab apples, pickles, and olives.

Dill-Dressed Chinese Cabbage

½ cup mayonnaise or salad dressing
¼ cup milk
3 tablespoons grated Parmesan cheese
1 tablespoon white wine vinegar
½ teaspoon dried dillweed
⅛ teaspoon garlic powder
Dash salt
Dash pepper
1 small head Chinese cabbage

In small mixing bowl combine mayonnaise or salad dressing, milk, Parmesan, wine vinegar, dillweed, garlic powder, salt, and pepper. Cut cabbage crosswise into thin slices; place on individual salad plates. Spoon mayonnaise mixture over. Serves 4.

Cheese-Sauced Broccoli

2 10-ounce packages frozen broccoli spears
½ cup mayonnaise or salad dressing
¼ cup shredded sharp process American cheese (1 ounce)
1 tablespoon milk

Cook broccoli according to package directions; drain. Meanwhile, in saucepan combine mayonnaise or salad dressing, shredded cheese, and milk; cook and stir over low heat till cheese melts. Serve cheese sauce over cooked broccoli. Serves 6 to 8.

Curried Cheese Sauce

Delicious served over broccoli or asparagus—

¼ cup milk
1 11-ounce can condensed Cheddar cheese soup
¼ teaspoon curry powder
2 tablespoons slivered almonds, toasted

In small saucepan gradually stir milk into cheese soup; stir in curry powder. Cook and stir till heated through. Serve over cooked vegetables; sprinkle with toasted almonds. Makes 1½ cups sauce.

Stir-Fried Green Beans

1 tablespoon cooking oil
1 9-ounce package frozen green beans, thawed
1 chicken bouillon cube
¼ cup boiling water
2 tablespoons sliced green onion
¼ teaspoon salt
1 teaspoon cornstarch

Heat oil in a 10-inch skillet. Add beans; cook, stirring frequently, 3 minutes. Dissolve bouillon in boiling water. Add to beans with onion and salt. Cover; cook till beans are tender, 3 to 5 minutes. Blend 1 tablespoon cold water into cornstarch; add to beans. Cook, stirring, till vegetables are coated. Makes 4 servings.

Zucchini with Walnuts

This unusual dish is shown on page 51—

1 pound zucchini, cut in ½-inch slices (about 4 cups)
⅓ cup sliced green onion with tops
2 tablespoons butter or margarine
3 tablespoons dry sherry
½ teaspoon salt
¼ cup coarsely chopped walnuts, toasted

In saucepan mix zucchini, onion, and butter. Cook, uncovered, over low heat for 5 minutes. Stir in wine and salt; cover and cook over low heat till zucchini is tender, 3 to 5 minutes. Add nuts. Serves 4.

Swiss-Dill Sauce

½ cup shredded process Swiss cheese
¼ cup mayonnaise or salad dressing
½ cup dairy sour cream
⅛ teaspoon dried dill weed

Mix cheese and mayonnaise. Cook and stir over low heat till cheese melts. (If necessary, beat smooth with rotary beater.) Stir in sour cream and dillweed; heat through. Serve over vegetables. Makes 1 cup.

Sour Cream Potatoes

A quick fix-up for instant potatoes—

**Packaged instant mashed potatoes
(enough for 2 servings)
¼ cup dairy sour cream
Milk
1 tablespoon sliced green onion tops**

Prepare instant mashed potatoes according to package directions, *except* omit milk and butter. Stir in dairy sour cream. With fork, beat in enough milk to make fluffy. Sprinkle with green onion tops. Serves 2.

Dilly Bread

A perfect accompaniment for soups—

**¼ cup butter or margarine, softened
½ teaspoon prepared mustard
¼ teaspoon dried dillweed
• • •
8 slices French bread**

Preheat broiler. In small mixing bowl combine softened butter or margarine, prepared mustard, and dried dillweed. Spread butter mixture on one side of French bread slices. Place bread slices, buttered side down, on baking sheet. Broil till golden, 1 to 2 minutes. Turn and broil 1 to 2 minutes longer. Makes 8 slices.

Parsley-Onion Bread

**1 tablespoon instant minced onion
1 tablespoon milk
¼ cup butter or margarine, softened
2 tablespoons snipped parsley
• • •
8 slices French bread**

Preheat broiler. In small mixing bowl combine instant minced onion and milk. Stir in softened butter or margarine and snipped parsley. Spread butter mixture on one side of French bread slices. Place bread slices, buttered side down, on baking sheet. Broil till golden, 1 to 2 minutes. Turn; broil 1 to 2 minutes more. Makes 8 slices.

Toasted Bun Sticks

Crisp breadsticks shown on page 51—

Preheat oven to 375°. Split 6 frankfurter buns lengthwise. Cut each bun half lengthwise (to make 24 sticks). Place on baking sheet. Brush each breadstick generously with Italian salad dressing, using about 1½ teaspoons for each. Bake at 375° till lightly browned, 10 to 12 minutes. Makes 24.

Herbed Biscuit Ring

**3 tablespoons butter, softened
1 teaspoon lemon juice
½ teaspoon celery seed
¼ teaspoon dried thyme, crushed
⅛ teaspoon rubbed sage
Dash paprika
1 package refrigerated biscuits
(10 biscuits)**

Preheat oven to 400°. Blend first 6 ingredients. Separate biscuits; spread tops with butter mixture. In 8 x 1½-inch round baking pan, arrange biscuits, buttered side up, to form ring; overlap slightly. Bake at 400° for 15 to 18 minutes. Serves 10.

Pineapple Brunch Cakes

**1 3-ounce package cream cheese,
softened
2 tablespoons sugar
1 egg
¼ teaspoon vanilla
1 8¼-ounce can crushed pineapple,
well drained
6 English muffins
¼ cup chopped pecans**

Preheat broiler. In small mixer bowl combine cheese and sugar. Beat in egg and vanilla; stir in pineapple. Split muffins; place on baking sheet and toast under broiler. Reduce oven to 375°. Spread pineapple mixture atop muffins, using about 1½ tablespoons mixture for each. Sprinkle with pecans. Bake at 375° for 6 to 8 minutes. Serve warm. Makes 12.

Eggnog Fondue

An interesting treat for the holiday season —

  1 3- or 3¼-ounce package *regular*
    vanilla pudding mix
1½ cups eggnog
  2 tablespoons light rum
    • • •
    Angel cake or pound cake, cut
      in bite-size pieces
    Bananas, cut in bite-size pieces

In medium saucepan combine vanilla pudding mix and eggnog. Cook, stirring constantly, till mixture thickens and bubbles. Stir in light rum. Transfer pudding mixture to fondue pot. Place over fondue burner. Spear cake or banana pieces with fondue fork; dip in fondue, swirling to coat. (If mixture becomes too thick, stir in a little additional eggnog.) Makes 4 servings.

Burgundy-Cherry Fondue

Use the blender to puree the mixture —

  1 21-ounce can cherry pie filling
  3 tablespoons red Burgundy
  4 teaspoons cornstarch
    Angel cake, cut in bite-size
      pieces

In blender container combine cherry pie filling, Burgundy, and cornstarch; cover and blend till mixture is pureed. Pour into saucepan; heat through. Transfer hot cherry mixture to fondue pot; place over fondue burner. Spear angel cake pieces with fondue fork; dip in fondue, swirling to coat. Makes 4 to 6 servings.

Tangy Strawberry Cooler

Yogurt contributes the tang —

  2 cups plain yogurt
  1 10-ounce package frozen
    strawberries, partially thawed

In blender container combine yogurt and strawberries. Cover; blend till foamy. Serve immediately. Makes 2 servings.

Jiffy Desserts

To many people, a meal isn't a meal without dessert. If that's the case with you, end the meal with one of these ideas:

● Fresh fruit with cheese is a delicious meal ending. Try apples, pears, grapes, and other fruit with cheeses such as Gouda, fontina, and Monterey Jack.

● Keep canned puddings on hand as the base for many delicious desserts. Try folding whipped dessert topping, tiny marshmallows, chopped nuts, or pieces of fruit into these puddings. Enhance the flavor of chocolate pudding by stirring in a little instant coffee powder or instant coffee crystals, crushed. Add a few chopped maraschino cherries to canned tapioca pudding. Spoon lemon pudding over slices of pound cake. Fold dairy sour cream into vanilla pudding.

● For quick strawberry shortcake, spoon frozen strawberries, thawed, over pound cake or angel cake slices. Top with whipped dessert topping.

● Fold crushed peanut brittle into whipped dessert topping and serve over pound cake or angel cake slices.

● Coat strawberries, grapes, or fresh pineapple cubes with sour cream or fruit-flavored yogurt. Then, sprinkle with brown sugar and/or flaked coconut.

● Combine orange marmalade and a dash of ground ginger, then drizzle over a mixture of fresh and/or canned fruits.

● Scoop vanilla ice cream onto a brownie and drizzle with chocolate syrup.

● Spoon marshmallow creme onto chocolate ice cream. Then, drizzle with chocolate syrup and top with chopped nuts.

● Layer strawberry ice cream and frozen strawberries, thawed, in parfait glasses.

● Drizzle your favorite liqueur over vanilla ice cream.

● Crumble coconut macaroons atop vanilla or chocolate ice cream. Top with your favorite ice cream topping.

● Spoon a little frozen lemonade concentrate, thawed, over a mixture of blueberries and peach slices.

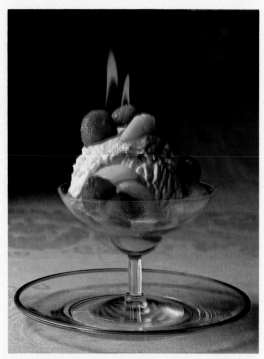

Frozen strawberries, canned peaches, and vanilla ice cream become company-special Strawberry-Peach Sundae *when you add rum and set aflame.*

Cranberry Jubilee
Subtly flavored with brandy—

¼ **cup sugar**
2 **teaspoons cornstarch**
½ **teaspoon ground cinnamon**
¼ **teaspoon ground nutmeg**
    Dash ground cloves
1 **16-ounce can whole cranberry**
    sauce
2 **tablespoons water**
¼ **cup brandy**
    Vanilla ice cream

In saucepan combine sugar, cornstarch, ground cinnamon, ground nutmeg, and ground cloves. Blend in cranberry sauce and water. Cook, stirring constantly, over medium heat till thickened and bubbly. Stir in 1 *tablespoon* of the brandy. Turn into chafing dish or heatproof bowl. Heat remaining brandy over low heat just till warm; flame and pour over cranberry mixture. Blend brandy into sauce; serve immediately over vanilla ice cream. Makes 2 cups sauce.

Mocha Toffee Parfaits
Crushed toffee bars add crunch to this layered dessert (shown on page 80)—

1 **tablespoon instant coffee crystals**
2 **tablespoons milk**
1 **18-ounce can vanilla pudding,**
    chilled
        • • •
½ **cup fudge topping**
2 **1⅛-ounce chocolate-covered English**
    toffee bars, coarsely crushed
    Whipped cream or frozen whipped
    dessert topping, thawed

Dissolve instant coffee crystals in milk. Stir into chilled vanilla pudding. Spoon *half* the pudding mixture into 4 parfait glasses. Top with *half* the fudge topping and *half* the crushed candy. Repeat layers in parfait glasses with remaining pudding mixture and remaining fudge topping. Top parfaits with whipped cream or whipped dessert topping and the remaining crushed candy. Makes 4 servings.

Strawberry-Peach Sundae
An elegant meal finale—

2 **tablespoons sugar**
1 **teaspoon cornstarch**
1 **10-ounce package frozen**
    strawberries, thawed
1 **8¾-ounce can peach slices,**
    drained
⅓ **cup rum**
    Vanilla ice cream

In small saucepan combine sugar and cornstarch; gradually stir in *half* the strawberries. Cook, stirring constantly, over medium heat till thickened and bubbly. Remove from heat. Stir in remaining strawberries and drained peach slices. Heat rum in ladle or small pan; flame and pour over fruit mixture. Serve over vanilla ice cream. Makes about 1½ cups sauce.

Coffee-Banana Smoothee

An interesting flavor blend—

½ cup light cream
2 ripe bananas, cut up
1 cup coffee ice cream, softened
1 tablespoon sugar
1 tablespoon instant coffee crystals
1 or 2 drops almond extract

Pour light cream into blender container; add cut up bananas, ice cream, sugar, instant coffee crystals, and almond extract. Cover blender; blend at high speed till mixture is thick and fluffy, a few seconds. Pour mixture into 2 or 3 chilled glasses. Serve immediately. Makes 2 or 3 servings.

Banana-Pineapple Shakes

A dessert you drink—

1 cup milk
2 small ripe bananas, cut up
½ of a 6-ounce can frozen pineapple
    juice concentrate, thawed (⅓ cup)
1 pint vanilla ice cream, softened

In blender container combine milk, bananas, and pineapple concentrate. Cover; blend till smooth. Add softened vanilla ice cream. Cover; blend just till smooth, a few seconds. Serve immediately. Serves 2 or 3.

Speedy Strawberry Parfaits

1 8-ounce carton plain yogurt
    (1 cup)
1 3-ounce package cream cheese,
    softened
¼ cup sugar
        • • •
1 21-ounce can strawberry pie
    filling
2 tablespoons chopped almonds,
    toasted

In small mixer bowl beat together yogurt, cheese, and sugar till smooth. In 6 parfait glasses alternately layer pie filling and yogurt mixture. Top with almonds. Serves 6.

Strawberry-Cheese Topping

Fruit-filled cake topping shown on the cover—

½ cup strawberry yogurt
1 4-ounce container whipped cream
    cheese
¼ cup sugar
1 cup fresh strawberries, halved
    Angel cake or pound cake

Stir yogurt into cream cheese till smooth. Stir in sugar. Fold in strawberries. Serve over cake slices. Makes 6 to 8 servings.

Pink Cream Dessert

Ice cream delicacy shown on page 51—

1 quart vanilla ice cream
⅓ cup crème d'almond
3 tablespoons crème de
    cacao
¼ cup chopped maraschino
    cherries (optional)

Spoon vanilla ice cream into blender container. Add crème d'almond and crème de cacao. Cover; blend just till smooth, a few seconds. Stir in chopped maraschino cherries, if desired. Pour mixture into dessert glasses. Serve immediately. Serves 4.

Butter-Rum Sundae

¼ cup butter or margarine
1 package creamy white frosting
    mix (for 2-layer cake)
2 tablespoons light corn syrup
⅓ cup evaporated milk
½ cup chopped pecans
¼ cup rum
    Vanilla ice cream

In saucepan heat and stir butter or margarine till browned; remove from heat. Blend in *about half* of the creamy white frosting mix and the corn syrup; add remaining frosting mix. Gradually stir in evaporated milk. Cook and stir till heated through. Remove from heat; stir in nuts and rum. Serve over ice cream. Makes 2 cups sauce.

Make It Easy

Do you dread meal preparation time because you're left with no time to relax? If so, start enjoying both. The recipes in this section are simple to prepare and require little attention while cooking. So, once the dish is on to cook, you can sit down and read the paper, have a cocktail, accomplish other tasks, converse with your guests, or leisurely prepare the rest of the meal.

You'll find many old favorites in this section, including spaghetti sauce, stews, soufflés, meat loaves, and soups. In addition, there are dozens of delicious recipes that are sure to become new favorites—baked chicken dishes, skillet meals, oven-roasted ribs, casseroles, baked desserts, and many more.

So, follow the advice given in the title of this section. Make dinner easily and then relax.

Put your oven to good use by roasting easy Orange-Glazed Ribs in it. The orange marmalade-ginger glaze complements the crispy pork spareribs. (See recipe, page 66.)

Main Dishes

Sweet Potato-Turkey Pie

2 tablespoons butter, melted
⅛ teaspoon ground nutmeg
⅛ teaspoon ground allspice
1 17-ounce can sweet potatoes,
   drained and mashed
½ cup fresh or frozen chopped onion
1 tablespoon butter or margarine
2 cups diced cooked turkey
1 10¾-ounce can condensed cream of
   mushroom soup
1 8-ounce can whole kernel corn,
   drained
1 8-ounce can peas, drained
1 small tomato, peeled and diced

Preheat oven to 350°. Beat first 3 ingredients and ¼ teaspoon salt into mashed sweet potatoes. Line a 9-inch pie plate with potato mixture, building up edges ½ inch high. Cook onion in 1 tablespoon butter till almost tender. Stir in turkey, soup, corn, peas, tomato, and ¼ teaspoon salt. Spoon into sweet potato shell. Bake at 350° for 35 minutes. Serves 6.

Baked Turkey Hash

1½ cups coarsely ground cooked turkey
1 cup cubed cooked potato
1 6-ounce can evaporated milk
¼ cup finely snipped parsley
¼ cup fresh or frozen chopped onion
1 teaspoon Worcestershire sauce
¼ teaspoon rubbed sage
¼ cup coarsely crushed saltine
   crackers
1 tablespoon butter, melted

Preheat oven to 350°. Stir together first 7 ingredients, ½ teaspoon salt, and dash pepper. Turn into lightly greased 1-quart casserole. Toss together crackers and butter; sprinkle atop casserole. Bake at 350° till heated through, about 30 minutes. Serves 4.

Chicken with Artichokes

4 medium whole chicken breasts,
   split, skinned, and boned
1 tablespoon cooking oil
   • • •
1 envelope spaghetti sauce mix
1 8-ounce can tomato sauce
½ cup dry sherry
1 3-ounce can sliced mushrooms,
   drained
1 9-ounce package frozen artichoke
   hearts, cooked and drained

Preheat oven to 350°. In skillet brown the chicken in hot oil. Meanwhile, combine sauce mix, tomato sauce, sherry, and ¼ cup water. Simmer 10 minutes; stir in mushrooms. Transfer chicken to 10x6x2-inch baking dish. Arrange artichokes around chicken; spoon sauce mixture over all. Bake, covered, at 350° for 45 minutes. Serves 4.

Chicken Pilaf

Preheat oven to 375°. In skillet brown 4 ready-to-cook chicken pieces in 2 tablespoons butter. Sprinkle with salt; remove from skillet. Cook and stir ⅓ cup long grain rice in skillet drippings till light golden. Add ⅔ cup water, ¼ cup fresh or frozen chopped onion, and 1 chicken bouillon cube; bring to boiling, stirring to dissolve bouillon. Stir in 2 tablespoons raisins and ¼ teaspoon salt. Turn into a 1-quart casserole. Top with browned chicken. Cover; bake at 375° till chicken and rice are tender, about 50 minutes. Serves 2.

Easy main dish

A sweet potato crust and saucy vegetable-turkey →
mixture combine to make Sweet Potato-Turkey Pie.
This entrée bakes in 35 minutes, while you relax.

Chicken-Rice Bake

A serving of this dish is shown on the cover—

>1 2½- to 3-pound ready-to-cook
>　broiler-fryer chicken, cut up
>2 tablespoons cooking oil
>1 7½-ounce can tomatoes, cut up
>⅔ cup uncooked long grain rice
>½ cup water
>½ cup chopped celery
>⅓ cup fresh or frozen chopped onion
>⅓ cup fresh or frozen chopped green
>　pepper
>¼ teaspoon rubbed sage
>　Paprika

Preheat oven to 350°. In skillet brown the chicken in hot oil. Meanwhile, combine undrained tomatoes, rice, water, celery, onion, green pepper, sage, ¾ teaspoon salt, and dash pepper; mix thoroughly. Turn into a 12x7½x2-inch baking dish. Arrange chicken atop rice mixture. Sprinkle with paprika, salt, and pepper. Cover; bake at 350° till chicken is tender, about 1 hour. Serves 4.

Peach-Glazed Chicken

>1 2½- to 3-pound ready-to-cook
>　broiler-fryer chicken, cut up
>　Paprika
>1 16-ounce can peach halves
>2 tablespoons lemon juice
>2 tablespoons soy sauce
>3 tablespoons butter or margarine
>1 tablespoon cornstarch

Preheat oven to 375°. Arrange chicken in 13x9x2-inch baking pan. Sprinkle with paprika and salt. Drain peaches; reserve ½ cup syrup. Combine reserved syrup, juice, and soy. Set aside 4 peach halves; mash remaining. Add mashed peaches to soy mixture; drizzle over chicken. Dot with butter. Bake, uncovered, at 375° for 45 minutes, basting often with sauce. Place reserved peaches in pan; bake 15 minutes more, basting often. Remove chicken and peaches to platter. Mix cornstarch and 2 tablespoons cold water; stir into pan juices. Cook and stir till thick; serve with chicken. Serves 4.

Cheese-Crumbed Cornish Hens

>2 Rock Cornish game hens, 14 to 16
>　ounces each (have meatman split
>　hens lengthwise)
>¼ cup sour cream dip with garlic
>1 cup finely crushed Cheddar cheese
>　crackers
>¼ teaspoon dried thyme, crushed
>　Dash pepper

Thaw hens in refrigerator. Preheat oven to 375°. Wash hens and pat dry. Coat well with dip. Mix crackers, thyme, and pepper. Roll hens in crumb mixture. Place, skin side up, in shallow baking pan. Bake at 375° till done, about 45 minutes. Makes 4 servings.

Crab-Stuffed Chicken Breasts

>6 whole chicken breasts,
>　skinned and boned
>½ cup chopped onion
>½ cup chopped celery
>5 tablespoons butter or margarine
>1 7½-ounce can crab meat, drained,
>　flaked, and cartilage removed
>½ cup herb-seasoned stuffing mix
>5 tablespoons dry white wine
>2 tablespoons all-purpose flour
>½ teaspoon paprika
>1 envelope hollandaise sauce mix
>　(enough for 1 cup sauce)
>¾ cup milk
>½ cup shredded process Swiss cheese

ENTERTAINING SPECIAL

Preheat oven to 375°. Pound chicken to flatten. Sprinkle with salt and pepper. Cook onion and celery in 3 *tablespoons* butter till tender. Remove from heat; add crab, stuffing mix, and 3 *tablespoons* wine; toss. Divide mixture among chicken pieces. Roll up and secure. Combine flour and paprika; coat chicken. Place in 12x7½x2-inch baking dish. Melt remaining butter; drizzle over chicken. Bake, uncovered, at 375° for 1 hour. Transfer to warm platter. Blend sauce mix and milk; cook and stir till thick. Add cheese and remaining wine; stir till cheese melts. Pour some sauce over chicken; pass remaining sauce. Serves 6.

Oven-baked Cheese-Crumbed Cornish Hens *get flavor and crispness from coating of sour cream dip and crushed Cheddar cheese crackers. Add color to the serving platter with watercress sprigs and cherry tomatoes.*

Baked Italian Chicken

Complete the menu with buttered zucchini, tossed salad, Italian bread, and ice cream—

½ cup water
½ cup chili sauce
½ teaspoon salt
½ teaspoon dried oregano, crushed
¼ teaspoon celery seed
⅛ teaspoon pepper
1 2½- to 3-pound ready-to-cook
    broiler-fryer chicken, cut up
½ cup fine dry bread crumbs
¼ cup butter or margarine

Preheat oven to 375°. Combine water, chili sauce, salt, oregano, celery seed, and pepper. Dip chicken in sauce mixture; coat skin side with crumbs. In 13x9x2-inch baking dish heat butter in oven till melted. Place chicken, crumb side up, in baking dish; pour on remaining sauce mixture. Bake at 375° till tender, about 1 hour. Serves 4.

Chicken-Wild Rice Skillet

1 cup sliced fresh mushrooms
1 small onion, sliced
½ cup chopped celery
¼ cup butter or margarine
• • •
2½ cups water
1 6-ounce package long grain and
    wild rice mix
8 slices cooked chicken (about 12
    ounces)
1 14½- or 15-ounce can asparagus
    spears, drained

In large skillet cook mushrooms, onion, and celery in butter or margarine till vegetables are tender but not brown. Add water and rice mix. Cover and bring to boiling. Reduce heat; simmer 25 minutes. Place chicken atop rice mixture; top with drained asparagus. Cook, covered, till heated through, about 5 minutes. Serves 4.

Cranberry-Wine Glazed Ham

    1 8-ounce can whole cranberry sauce
    ⅓ cup packed brown sugar
    ¼ cup dry red wine
    1 teaspoon prepared mustard
    1 1½-pound canned ham
      Whole cloves

Preheat oven to 325°. In saucepan combine cranberry sauce, brown sugar, wine, and mustard; simmer, uncovered, for 5 minutes. Place ham on rack in shallow baking pan. Score top in diamond pattern; stud with cloves. Bake at 325° till meat thermometer registers 140°, 45 to 50 minutes; brush occasionally with cranberry mixture. Pass the remaining cranberry mixture with the ham. Makes 6 servings.

Apple-Raisin Topped Ham

    1 21-ounce can apple pie filling
    ⅓ cup raisins
    ⅓ cup orange juice
    ¼ cup chopped pecans
    1 tablespoon lemon juice
    ¼ teaspoon ground cinnamon
    1 1½-pound fully cooked ham slice
      (about ¾ inch thick)

Preheat oven to 350°. Combine apple pie filling, raisins, orange juice, chopped pecans, lemon juice, and cinnamon. Turn into 12x7½x2-inch baking dish. Place ham atop. Cover; bake at 350° till heated through, about 40 minutes. Makes 6 servings.

Build Nutrition into Meals

Make meals both exciting and nutritious. Follow the Basic Four Food Groups (see page 84) as guides, but remember not to typecast foods. For instance, use milk in soups and desserts as well as in beverages. Feature fruit as an appetizer or dessert. Include vegetables in main-dish casseroles, salads, and sandwiches.

Ham-Potato Bake

This tasty casserole is shown on page 80—

    2 15- or 16-ounce cans sliced
      potatoes, drained
    2 medium carrots, shredded (1 cup)
    1½ cups cubed fully cooked ham
    1 10¾-ounce can condensed cream
      of mushroom soup
    1 cup shredded sharp process
      American cheese (4 ounces)
    ¼ cup milk
    1 tablespoon instant minced onion
    ⅛ teaspoon pepper
    1 cup soft bread crumbs
    1 tablespoon butter or margarine,
      melted

Preheat oven to 350°. Place *half* the potatoes and *half* the carrots in 2-quart casserole. Combine ham, soup, ½ cup of the cheese, milk, onion, and pepper. Pour *half* of the soup mixture over the potatoes. Repeat layers. Combine crumbs, remaining cheese, and butter; sprinkle over the casserole. Bake at 350° till heated through, about 45 minutes. Serves 4 to 6.

Ham Stuffing Casserole

    ¼ cup fresh or frozen chopped onion
    ¼ cup butter or margarine
    2 cups herb-seasoned stuffing mix
    2 cups diced fully cooked ham
    1 large apple, peeled and chopped
    4 slightly beaten eggs
    1½ cups milk
    1 11-ounce can condensed Cheddar
      cheese soup
    ¼ cup milk

Preheat oven to 350°. In saucepan cook onion in butter till tender; add stuffing mix, ham, and apple. Combine eggs and 1½ cups milk; stir into stuffing mixture. Spoon into 8x8x2-inch baking dish. Bake at 350° for 40 minutes. Let stand 5 minutes; cut in squares. Meanwhile, in saucepan combine cheese soup and ¼ cup milk. Cook and stir over low heat till heated through. Serve over casserole. Makes 6 servings.

Applesauce-Pork Loaf

1 slightly beaten egg
1 cup soft bread crumbs (1¼ slices bread)
1 8½-ounce can applesauce
2 tablespoons fresh or frozen chopped onion
2 teaspoons Dijon-style mustard
1 teaspoon snipped parsley
¼ teaspoon salt
Dash pepper
½ pound bulk pork sausage
½ pound fully cooked ham, ground
1 tablespoon packed brown sugar
1 tablespoon vinegar

Preheat oven to 350°. In bowl combine egg, crumbs, ½ cup applesauce, onion, 1 *teaspoon* mustard, parsley, salt, and pepper. Add meats; mix well. Shape into a round loaf 8 inches in diameter in a baking pan. With a spoon, make a depression in top of the loaf. Combine the remaining applesauce, brown sugar, vinegar, and remaining mustard; pour into depression. Bake at 350° for 1 hour. Makes 4 servings.

Pork Steak-Vegetable Bake

4 medium potatoes, peeled and cut lengthwise in ¼-inch slices
1 large carrot, sliced
4 pork steaks, cut ½ inch thick
½ cup water
½ envelope onion soup mix (¼ cup)
2 tablespoons soy sauce

Preheat oven to 350°. Place potatoes and carrot slices in bottom of 12x7½x2-inch baking dish. Trim fat from steaks. In large skillet cook trimmings till about 2 tablespoons fat accumulate; discard trimmings. In hot fat brown the steaks well on both sides. In small saucepan combine water, onion soup mix, and soy sauce; bring to boiling. Spoon *half* of the soup mixture over the potatoes and carrots; top with pork steaks. Spoon remaining soup mixture over. Cover; bake at 350° for 1 hour. Uncover and bake 10 minutes more. Makes 4 servings.

Polynesian Pork Steaks

6 pork steaks
1 4¾-ounce jar strained plums (baby food)
¼ cup flaked coconut
2 tablespoons water
1 tablespoon vinegar
1 tablespoon cooking oil
2 teaspoons soy sauce
½ teaspoon salt
½ teaspoon ground ginger
½ teaspoon grated lemon peel
Dash pepper

Trim fat from steaks. In large skillet cook trimmings till about 2 tablespoons fat accumulate; discard trimmings. Brown the steaks in hot fat. Season steaks generously with salt. Combine plums, coconut, water, vinegar, cooking oil, soy sauce, ½ teaspoon salt, ginger, lemon peel, and pepper; pour over steaks. Cover; simmer till tender, 35 to 40 minutes. Remove meat to warm platter; spoon sauce over. Makes 6 servings.

Pennsylvania Dutch Pork Chops

A tasty skillet dinner for two —

2 pork shoulder chops, cut ½ inch thick
1 8-ounce can sauerkraut, drained, rinsed, and snipped
½ teaspoon caraway seed
¼ cup water
• • •
½ cup applesauce
2 tablespoons fresh or frozen chopped onion
1 tablespoon packed brown sugar

Trim fat from chops. In skillet cook trimmings till about 1 tablespoon fat accumulates; discard trimmings. Brown the chops in hot fat. Remove chops from skillet; drain off fat. Combine sauerkraut and caraway seed in skillet; add water. Place chops atop. Season well with salt and pepper. Combine applesauce, onion, and brown sugar; pile atop chops. Cover; simmer till done, about 35 minutes. Makes 2 servings.

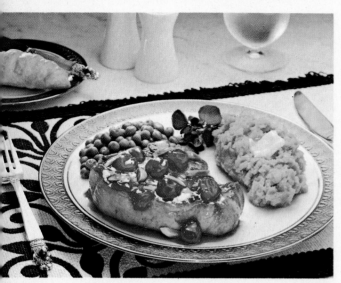

Lean and luscious Cherry-Glazed Pork Chops *are an elegant yet easy entrée for the hostess who wants to prepare a special dinner for two after five.*

Cherry-Glazed Pork Chops

  2 pork chops
  ¼ cup cherry preserves
  1 tablespoon light corn syrup
  1 tablespoon red wine vinegar
    Dash salt
    Dash ground cinnamon
    Dash ground nutmeg
    Dash ground cloves
  1 tablespoon slivered almonds,
      toasted

In skillet brown chops on both sides. Drain off fat. Sprinkle chops with a little salt and pepper. Add 1 tablespoon water. Cover; cook over low heat for 30 minutes. Meanwhile, in small saucepan combine preserves, corn syrup, vinegar, dash salt, cinnamon, nutmeg, and cloves. Heat mixture to boiling, stirring frequently. Remove from heat; stir in almonds. Keep warm till ready to use. When chops have cooked 30 minutes, spoon on just enough sauce to glaze; cover and cook till chops are tender, about 15 minutes more, basting once or twice with remaining sauce. Makes 2 servings.

Orange-Glazed Ribs

These flavorful ribs are shown on page 58—

  4 pounds pork spareribs
  ⅔ cup orange marmalade
  3 tablespoons soy sauce
  2 tablespoons lemon juice
  ¾ teaspoon ground ginger

Preheat oven to 450°. Place ribs, meaty side down, in shallow roasting pan. Bake at 450° for 30 minutes. Remove from oven; drain off excess fat. Turn ribs meaty side up. Reduce oven temperature to 350°; continue baking 30 minutes more. Combine marmalade, soy sauce, lemon juice, and ginger; spoon *half* of the sauce over the ribs. Bake 30 minutes more, spooning remaining sauce over occasionally. Garnish with orange slices, if desired. Makes 4 servings.

Veal Paprikash

  2 tablespoons all-purpose flour
  ½ teaspoon salt
  1 pound veal round steak, cut in
      ¾-inch cubes
  2 tablespoons cooking oil
  1¼ cups water
  1 tablespoon instant minced onion
  1 tablespoon paprika
  1 5½-ounce package noodles with
      sour cream sauce mix
  ¼ cup water
  1 tablespoon butter or margarine
  1½ teaspoons poppy seed

Combine flour, salt, and dash pepper. Coat veal with flour mixture. In large skillet slowly brown the veal on all sides in hot oil. Add the 1¼ cups water, onion, and paprika. Cover and cook over low heat till veal is tender, about 45 minutes, stirring occasionally. Blend sauce mix from noodle package with the ¼ cup water. Stir into meat mixture; cook over low heat about 5 minutes more, stirring frequently. Meanwhile, cook noodles according to package directions; drain thoroughly. Toss with butter and poppy seed. Turn noodles onto warm platter; top with veal mixture. Serves 4 or 5.

Oven Hamburgers

¾ cup soft bread crumbs (1 slice)
1 11-ounce can condensed Cheddar
   cheese soup
1½ pounds lean ground beef
¼ cup chili sauce
2 teaspoons prepared mustard
   Hot cooked noodles

Preheat oven to 350°. Combine crumbs, ½
cup of the soup, and ½ teaspoon salt. Add
ground beef and mix well; shape into 6
patties. Place in 11x7½x1½-inch baking
pan. Blend together remaining soup, chili
sauce, and mustard; pour over patties. Bake,
covered, at 350° till done, about 45 minutes.
Serve patties on noodles. Stir sauce and
spoon over patties. Makes 6 servings.

Beef Oven Stew

*For unexpected company, double this recipe
and bake in a 2½-quart casserole—*

1 beaten egg
2 tablespoons cornmeal
2 teaspoons instant minced onion
½ teaspoon dry mustard
¼ teaspoon chili powder
½ pound ground beef
1 tablespoon cooking oil
2 small potatoes, peeled and
   quartered
2 small carrots, sliced
1 small onion, quartered
2 teaspoons all-purpose flour
1 8-ounce can tomatoes
1 beef bouillon cube

Preheat oven to 350°. Combine egg, cornmeal, instant onion, mustard, chili powder,
and ½ teaspoon salt. Add beef; mix well.
Shape into 6 balls. Brown in hot oil. Place
meatballs in 1½-quart casserole. Add potatoes, carrots, and quartered onion. Sprinkle with salt and pepper. Blend flour into
drippings in skillet. Add tomatoes, bouillon
cube, and 2 tablespoons water. Cook and
stir till bubbly. Pour over meat and vegetables. Cover; bake at 350° till vegetables
are tender, about 1 hour. Makes 2 servings.

Meat Loaf Skillet Supper

1 slightly beaten egg
¼ cup fine dry bread crumbs
¼ cup fresh or frozen chopped onion
1 tablespoon snipped parsley
½ teaspoon salt
   Dash pepper
1 pound ground beef
1 tablespoon cooking oil
1 10-ounce package frozen mixed
   vegetables
1 8-ounce can tomatoes, cut up
2 tablespoons all-purpose flour

Combine egg, bread crumbs, onion, parsley,
salt, pepper, and ¼ cup water. Add ground
meat and mix thoroughly. Shape into a
6x3½-inch loaf. In skillet brown the meat
in hot oil. Spoon off excess fat. Add mixed
vegetables and tomatoes. Cook, covered,
about 45 minutes. Remove meat to serving
platter and keep warm. Combine flour and
1 cup cold water; stir into vegetables. Cook
and stir till thickened and bubbly. Season
to taste. Serve with meat. Makes 4 servings.

Chinese Stew

1½ pounds beef stew meat, cut in
   1-inch cubes
2 tablespoons cornstarch
¼ teaspoon ground ginger
⅛ teaspoon pepper
1 tablespoon cooking oil
2 cups water
1 10½-ounce can condensed golden
   mushroom soup
1 small onion, thinly sliced
2 tablespoons soy sauce
1 small head Chinese cabbage, cut
   in 1-inch cubes (4 cups)
1 8-ounce can bamboo shoots, drained

Coat meat with cornstarch; sprinkle with
ginger and pepper. In large skillet brown
the meat in hot oil. Combine water, soup,
onion, and soy sauce. Add to meat. Cover
and simmer till tender, about 1½ hours.
Add cabbage and bamboo shoots; cover and
simmer 5 to 8 minutes more. Serves 6.

Oriental Stuffed Steaks

1 6-ounce package long
   grain and wild rice mix
1 slightly beaten egg
¼ cup sliced green onion with tops
6 beef strip steaks
¼ to ½ cup bottled teriyaki sauce

Cook rice mix according to package directions till done, about 25 minutes. Cool slightly; stir in egg and onion.

Preheat broiler. Using a sharp knife, cut a pocket in each steak. Stuff with rice mixture. Broil steaks 4 inches from the heat till desired doneness. (Allow 4 to 6 minutes on each side for medium-rare.) Brush often with teriyaki sauce. Garnish with mushrooms and watercress, if desired. Serves 6.

Mexican Style Steak

1½ pounds beef round steak, cut in
   serving-size pieces
⅛ teaspoon garlic powder
2 tablespoons shortening
1 15-ounce can tamales in sauce
1 10-ounce can enchilada sauce

Pound steak on both sides; sprinkle with garlic powder. In skillet brown steak in hot shortening. Drain off fat. Drain tamales, reserving sauce. Unwrap tamales and cut in thirds; set aside. Combine reserved tamale sauce, enchilada sauce, and ¼ cup water. Pour over steak in skillet. Cover, simmer till meat is tender, about 45 minutes. Add tamale pieces and cook 10 minutes more. Makes 6 servings.

Remember elegant Oriental Stuffed Steaks when you need an extraordinary main dish. The thick, juicy strip steaks are stuffed with a long grain and wild rice mixture and then basted with teriyaki sauce while broiling.

Swiss and Frank Pie

A variation of the classic Quiche Lorraine—

  1 unbaked 9-inch pastry shell
  ¼ cup fresh or frozen chopped onion
  1 tablespoon butter or margarine
  2 cups thinly sliced frankfurters
      (5 or 6 frankfurters)
  1 cup shredded process Swiss cheese
      (4 ounces)
        • • •
  3 slightly beaten eggs
  1½ cups milk
  1 teaspoon dry mustard
  ½ teaspoon salt
  ¼ teaspoon ground nutmeg
      Dash pepper

Preheat oven to 450°. Bake pastry shell at
450° just till lightly browned, about 7 minutes. Remove from oven. Reduce oven temperature to 325°. Meanwhile, in a small
skillet cook onion in butter or margarine
till tender but not brown. Place sliced
frankfurters, shredded Swiss cheese, and
cooked onion in baked pastry shell. In bowl
combine eggs, milk, dry mustard, salt,
ground nutmeg, and pepper. Pour egg mixture over frankfurter-cheese mixture. Bake
pie at 325° till almost set in the center, 35
to 40 minutes. Let set 10 to 15 minutes
before serving. Cut into wedges. Serves 6.

Frank-Macaroni Skillet

  2½ cups water
  1 8-ounce can tomato sauce
  1 envelope spaghetti sauce mix
  1 cup uncooked macaroni (half of a
      7-ounce package)
  4 or 5 frankfurters, cut in 1-inch
      pieces
  1½ teaspoons Worcestershire sauce

In large saucepan combine water, tomato
sauce, and spaghetti sauce mix. Bring to
boiling; stir in macaroni. Cover and cook
over low heat till macaroni is tender, 15
to 20 minutes, stirring frequently. Stir in
frankfurters and Worcestershire sauce; cook
till heated through. Makes 4 servings.

How to Cook Pasta

Use a large pan filled with plenty of
water to cook spaghetti, noodles, macaroni, and other pasta. For 8 ounces of
any of these, use at least three quarts of
water. For seasoning, add 1 teaspoon
salt for each quart of water. To prevent
the pasta from sticking together and the
water from boiling over, add a teaspoon
of cooking oil to the water.

Bring the salted water to a vigorous
boil, then add the pasta. (Don't break
long spaghetti. Instead dip one end in
the water and curl the spaghetti around
the pan as it softens.) Keep the water
boiling constantly and stir at first to
prevent sticking. Cook, uncovered, till
the pasta is tender but still firm. Drain
immediately when cooked.

Plan to serve 4 or 5 from 8 ounces
spaghetti and 8 from 8 ounces noodles.

Spaghetti Sauce

  1 pound ground beef
  ½ pound Italian sausage
  1 28-ounce can tomatoes, cut up
  1 15-ounce can tomato sauce
  1 cup dry red wine
  ¾ cup fresh or frozen chopped onion
  ¼ cup snipped parsley
  1 clove garlic, minced
  1 teaspoon dried oregano, crushed
  ¼ teaspoon dried thyme, crushed
  1 bay leaf
  1 6-ounce can sliced mushrooms,
      drained
      Hot cooked spaghetti

In Dutch oven cook ground beef and sausage
till browned; drain off excess fat. Stir in
tomatoes, tomato sauce, wine, onion, parsley, garlic, oregano, thyme, and bay leaf.
Bring to boiling; simmer, uncovered, for
1 hour, stirring occasionally. Season with
salt to taste. Add mushrooms; simmer 15
minutes longer. Remove bay leaf. Serve
over hot spaghetti. Makes 6 servings.

Save Chopping Time

Cut last-minute preparation time by chopping several onions and green peppers at one time, then freezing them. So that you can use them without remeasuring, freeze the chopped vegetables in recipe-size portions, such as ¼ or ½ cup. Use frozen portions within 1 month.

Sausage-Macaroni Skillet

    ½ pound bulk pork sausage
    ¼ cup fresh or frozen chopped green
        pepper
    2 tablespoons fresh or frozen
        chopped onion
    1 8-ounce can tomato sauce
    ½ cup elbow macaroni
    1 teaspoon sugar
    ¼ to ½ teaspoon chili powder
    ¼ cup dairy sour cream

In skillet lightly brown the sausage. Add green pepper and onion. Cook till vegetables are tender. Drain off fat. Stir in tomato sauce, macaroni, sugar, chili powder, ¾ cup water, and ¼ teaspoon salt. Cover; simmer till macaroni is done, about 20 minutes. Blend in sour cream. Heat through but *do not boil*. Makes 2 servings.

Sausage-Potato Supper

Using one 4⅝- or 5½-ounce package dry scalloped potato mix, in skillet combine dry potatoes and seasoned sauce mix from the package. Stir in water *to equal total liquid* called for on package. Heat to boiling, stirring occasionally. Reduce heat; simmer, covered, till potatoes are tender, about 30 minutes. Stir in one 16-ounce can sauerkraut, drained. Sprinkle with ½ teaspoon caraway seed. Arrange one 12-ounce package smoked pork sausage links spoke-fashion atop the vegetable mixture. Cover; cook till sausages are heated through, about 10 minutes. Serves 4.

Cheese-Stuffed Manicotti

This tasty pasta dish is shown on the cover—

    6 manicotti shells
    1½ cups shredded mozzarella cheese
        (6 ounces)
    1 cup cream-style cottage cheese
    ⅓ cup grated Parmesan cheese
    2 beaten eggs
    ¼ cup snipped parsley
    1 teaspoon instant minced onion
    1 15-ounce can spaghetti sauce with
        mushrooms
    ⅓ cup water

Preheat oven to 350°. Cook manicotti according to package directions till tender. Drain. Meanwhile, combine ¾ cup mozzarella, the cottage cheese, and Parmesan. Stir in eggs, parsley, and onion. Combine spaghetti sauce and water; pour ⅔ cup sauce mixture into 10x6x2-inch baking dish. Split manicotti shells lengthwise with kitchen shears. Open and fill with cheese mixture, using about ¼ cup for each shell. Close. Arrange in baking dish. Pour remaining sauce over. Sprinkle with remaining mozzarella. Bake, uncovered, at 350° till bubbly and heated through, about 35 minutes. Serves 3.

Swiss Cheese Bake

    1 cup shredded process Swiss cheese
        (4 ounces)
    1 4½-ounce can deviled ham
    1 tablespoon prepared mustard
    8 slices white bread, toasted
    2 cups milk
    4 slightly beaten eggs
    1 teaspoon sesame seed

Preheat oven to 325°. Mix cheese, deviled ham, and mustard. Spread mixture on 4 *slices* toast, using about ½ cup for each slice. Top with remaining toast. Quarter sandwiches diagonally; arrange in three rows in 10x6x2-inch baking dish, standing *crust side down*. Beat together milk and eggs; pour over the sandwiches. Sprinkle sesame seed over top. Bake at 325° for 50 to 55 minutes. Makes 5 or 6 servings.

Shrimp-Macaroni Casserole

1 7¼- or 8-ounce package macaroni
   and cheese dinner mix
½ cup milk
2 10½-ounce cans condensed cream of
   chicken soup
2 4½-ounce cans shrimp, drained
½ teaspoon Worcestershire sauce
½ cup bite-size shredded rice squares,
   coarsely crushed
1 tablespoon butter or margarine,
   melted

Preheat oven to 350°. Prepare macaroni and cheese mix according to package directions, *except* use the ½ cup milk. Stir in soup, shrimp, Worcestershire, and dash pepper. Turn into 2-quart casserole. Toss together crushed cereal and melted butter or margarine. Sprinkle over casserole. Bake at 350° about 45 minutes. Makes 6 servings.

Combine convenience foods in Shrimp-Macaroni Casserole. *This pantry-shelf special uses macaroni and cheese mix and canned soup and shrimp.*

Cheese-Mushroom Soufflé

2 tablespoons butter or margarine
1 cup shredded sharp process
   American cheese (4 ounces)
1 10¾-ounce can condensed cream
   of mushroom soup
1½ cups soft bread crumbs
¼ cup milk
4 egg yolks
4 egg whites
⅓ cup milk

Preheat oven to 350°. In large saucepan melt butter; add cheese. Cook and stir over low heat till cheese melts. Add *half* the soup, bread crumbs, and ¼ cup milk; stir till blended. Remove from heat. Beat egg yolks till thick and lemon-colored; gradually stir in hot mixture. Wash and dry beaters. Beat egg whites till stiff peaks form; fold in egg yolk mixture. Turn into *ungreased* 10x6x2-inch baking dish. Bake at 350° till knife inserted just off-center comes out clean, 25 to 30 minutes.

    Meanwhile, for sauce stir together remaining soup and ⅓ cup milk. Heat through. Serve with soufflé. Serves 4 to 6.

Shrimp-Stuffed Fish

1 3-pound fresh or frozen whitefish
   or other fish, boned and dressed
½ cup chopped celery
¼ cup fresh or frozen chopped green
   pepper
¼ cup fresh or frozen chopped onion
6 tablespoons butter or margarine
2 cups corn bread stuffing mix
1 4½-ounce can shrimp, drained
¼ cup mayonnaise
1 tablespoon snipped parsley
   Dash cayenne
1 tablespoon cooking oil

Thaw frozen fish. Preheat oven to 350°. Pat fish dry; sprinkle inside generously with salt. Place in greased shallow baking pan. Cook celery, green pepper, and onion in butter till tender. Stir in stuffing mix and ⅓ cup water. Add shrimp, mayonnaise, parsley, and cayenne; mix. Stuff loosely into fish. (Bake extra stuffing in covered casserole for 30 minutes.) Brush fish with oil. Cover; bake at 350° till fish flakes easily, 45 to 60 minutes. Makes 8 servings.

Bratwurst Sandwiches

Simmered in beer for a delightful flavor—

6 bratwurst links (12 ounces)
1 8-ounce can sauerkraut, drained
    and snipped
1 cup beer
2 teaspoons instant minced onion
1 teaspoon caraway seed
6 frankfurter buns, split and
    toasted

Place bratwurst links in large saucepan. Combine snipped sauerkraut, beer, instant minced onion, and caraway seed. Spoon mixture over sausage links. Cover; simmer for 30 minutes. Place bratwurst links in toasted frankfurter buns; spoon sauerkraut mixture over bratwurst links. Serves 6.

Hot Corned Beef Buns

2 cups finely shredded cabbage
1 12-ounce can corned beef, crumbled
½ cup mayonnaise or salad dressing
1 teaspoon instant minced onion
1 teaspoon horseradish mustard
8 hamburger buns, split and
    buttered
16 dill pickle slices

Preheat oven to 375°. Combine cabbage, corned beef, mayonnaise, minced onion, and horseradish mustard. Spread about ⅓ cup filling on bottom half of each hamburger bun; top each with two pickle slices and the other half of bun. Wrap individually in foil. Place on baking sheet. Bake at 375° till hot, about 20 minutes. Makes 8 servings.

Simmer up a potful of Hearty Chicken Soup *for supper after your day's work is done. No time to stew a chicken? Use canned chicken for meatiness, and add vegetables and herbs to give the soup distinctive flavor.*

Hearty Chicken Soup

Use either canned chicken or leftover cooked chicken to prepare this flavorful soup—

3 cups water
1 16-ounce can tomatoes, cut up
1 carrot, sliced (½ cup)
1 small onion, sliced (½ cup)
½ cup sliced celery
1 teaspoon salt
¼ teaspoon dried thyme, crushed
1 bay leaf

• • •

2 5-ounce cans boned chicken, cut
up *or* 1½ cups diced cooked
chicken
1 cup uncooked medium noodles
1 3-ounce can sliced mushrooms,
drained

In large saucepan combine water, tomatoes, sliced carrot, onion, celery, salt, thyme, and bay leaf. Bring mixture to boiling; reduce heat. Simmer, covered, for 30 minutes. Remove bay leaf. Stir in diced chicken, uncooked noodles, and drained mushrooms. Boil gently, covered, till noodles are done, 8 to 10 minutes. Makes 5 or 6 servings.

Beef-Cabbage Soup

Serve buttered rye bread and dill pickle strips with this soup—

2 cups coarsely chopped cabbage
1 16-ounce can tomatoes, cut up
1½ cups water
1 tablespoon instant minced onion
1 teaspoon instant beef bouillon
granules
1 teaspoon sugar
⅛ teaspoon pepper
1 12-ounce can corned beef, broken
into chunks

In large saucepan combine chopped cabbage, tomatoes, water, instant minced onion, beef bouillon granules, sugar, and pepper. Bring the mixture to boiling; reduce heat. Simmer, covered, till cabbage is tender, about 30 minutes. Stir in corned beef chunks; heat through. Serves 4 or 5.

Vegetable Chili

1 pound ground beef
1 cup fresh or frozen chopped onion
1 16-ounce can tomatoes, cut up
1 10-ounce package frozen mixed
vegetables
1 8-ounce can tomato sauce
¾ cup water
1 to 2 teaspoons chili powder
1 teaspoon salt

In saucepan cook beef and onion till beef is browned. Drain off fat. Stir in remaining ingredients. Cover; simmer till vegetables are done, about 40 minutes. Serves 4.

Beef-Corn Stew

1 pound ground beef
½ cup fresh or frozen chopped onion
3 large potatoes, peeled and diced
1 17-ounce can cream-style corn
1 10½-ounce can condensed beef
broth

In large skillet brown beef and onion; drain off fat. Add remaining ingredients, 1 teaspoon salt, and dash pepper; mix well. Cover; cook over low heat for 20 to 25 minutes, stirring occasionally. Serves 4.

Easy Vegetable Soup

2 13¾-ounce cans chicken broth
(3½ cups)
1 10-ounce package frozen mixed
Italian *or* Spanish vegetables
⅓ cup catsup
¼ cup anellini (tiny hollow pasta
circles) or macaroni
2 tablespoons dried celery flakes
1 tablespoon instant minced onion
1 teaspoon Italian salad dressing
mix

In large saucepan combine all ingredients. Bring to boiling; reduce heat. Cover and simmer till pasta is tender, about 30 minutes. Makes 5 or 6 servings.

Side Dishes and Desserts

Sangria Acapulco

½ orange
¼ cup sugar
1 ⅘-quart bottle dry red wine
⅔ cup orange-flavored liqueur
1 7-ounce bottle club soda
Cracked ice

Thinly slice outer peel from orange with vegetable peeler. Put peel in large pitcher with sugar. Bruise peel with back of spoon to release oils. Add wine and liqueur. Chill 15 minutes. Remove peel. Add soda. Garnish with thin orange slices, if desired. Serve in glasses with ice. Serves 6.

Deviled Nuts

1½ cups pecan halves (5 ounces)
1½ cups whole blanched almonds
    (8 ounces)
1 tablespoon butter, melted
1 tablespoon cooking oil
2 teaspoons celery salt
1½ teaspoons chili powder

Preheat oven to 300°. Place nuts in 13x9x2-inch baking pan. Mix remaining ingredients and 1 teaspoon salt. Drizzle over nuts; stir to coat. Bake at 300° till almonds are lightly browned, 25 to 30 minutes; stir often. Serve warm or cool. Makes 3 cups.

Creamy Lime Dressing

1 8-ounce carton plain yogurt
2 tablespoons honey
1 tablespoon syrup from canned
    fruit *or* milk
1 teaspoon grated lime peel

Combine all ingredients and dash salt; chill quickly in the freezer. Serve over fresh or canned fruit salad. Makes 1 cup dressing.

Fiesta Corn Bake

1 17-ounce can cream-style corn
1 8¼-ounce can sliced carrots,
    drained (1 cup)
¼ cup fresh or frozen chopped onion
¼ cup sliced pitted ripe olives
1 tablespoon snipped parsley
1¾ cups soft bread crumbs (3 slices)
2 beaten eggs
½ teaspoon salt
    Dash pepper
    Dash bottled hot pepper sauce
1 tablespoon butter or margarine,
    melted

Preheat oven to 350°. Combine corn, carrots, onion, olives, and parsley. Add 1 cup of the bread crumbs, eggs, salt, pepper, and hot pepper sauce. Pour into a 10x6x2-inch baking dish. Toss remaining crumbs with butter; sprinkle atop casserole. Bake at 350° for 40 minutes. Remove from oven; let stand 5 minutes before serving. Serves 6.

Peppy Potatoes

1 2⅜-ounce package seasoned coating
    mix for chicken
4 unpeeled potatoes, cut in 1-inch
    wedges
    Butter or margarine, melted

Preheat oven to 325°. Pour coating mix and ¼ teaspoon salt into a bag. Dip potatoes in butter; shake a few at a time in coating mixture. Place on greased baking sheet. Bake at 325° for 60 minutes. Serves 4.

Special touches made easy

Side dishes and desserts that fit after work schedules →
include Fiesta Corn Bake, Crab Apple-Peach Dumplings *(see recipe, page 79), and* Deviled Nuts.

Six generous servings of Apple-Filled Squash are apple-pie easy to make when you add sugar and spice to canned pie-sliced fruit for the tasty filling.

Potato-Vegetable Scallop

A tasty way to dress up scalloped potatoes—

- 1 4⅝- or 5½-ounce package dry scalloped potato mix
- 1 10-ounce package frozen mixed vegetables
- ½ cup thinly sliced onion
- ¼ teaspoon celery seed
- 2½ cups boiling water
- 2 tablespoons butter or margarine
- ½ cup shredded sharp process American cheese (2 ounces)

Preheat oven to 400°. Place dried potatoes from mix in 1½-quart casserole. Sprinkle with the envelope of sauce mix from package. Top with frozen mixed vegetables, sliced onion, and celery seed. Pour boiling water over all; stir till well combined. Dot with butter or margarine. Cover; bake at 400° till potatoes are tender, about 35 minutes. Uncover; sprinkle with shredded cheese. Return to oven till cheese melts, 2 to 3 minutes more. Makes 6 servings.

Apple-Filled Squash

- 3 acorn squash
- 5 tablespoons butter or margarine, melted
- 1 18-ounce can pie-sliced apples
- ¾ cup packed brown sugar
- 1 teaspoon lemon juice
- ¼ teaspoon ground ginger

Preheat oven to 350°. Halve squash lengthwise; remove seeds. Brush with 2 *tablespoons* of the butter and sprinkle with salt. Place, cut side down, in large baking dish. Bake at 350° for 35 minutes. Combine apples, brown sugar, lemon juice, and ginger. Turn squash cut side up in baking dish. Fill centers with apple mixture. Drizzle with remaining butter. Continue baking till tender, about 25 minutes more. If desired, sprinkle with ground cinnamon. Serves 6.

Rice Pilaf

- 1½ cups uncooked long grain rice
- ¼ cup fresh or frozen finely chopped onion
- 3 tablespoons butter or margarine
- 1 13¾-ounce can chicken broth
- 1 cup water
- ½ teaspoon salt

In a 10-inch skillet cook rice and chopped onion in butter or margarine until rice is golden, stirring often. Add chicken broth, water, and salt. Bring to boiling; reduce heat. Cover and simmer till rice is tender, about 15 minutes. Fluff up with a fork. Makes 8 servings.

Parslied Carrots

Preheat oven to 400°. Halve 8 medium carrots lengthwise. Place in a 10x6x2-inch baking dish. Stir in 2 tablespoons water, 2 tablespoons butter, 1 teaspoon sugar, ¼ teaspoon salt, and dash pepper. Cover tightly with foil; bake at 400° till tender, 45 to 50 minutes. Sprinkle with 2 teaspoons snipped parsley. Serves 4 to 6.

Cranberry Ring

Perfect for a weekend brunch—

    ½ cup cranberry-orange relish
    1 tablespoon light corn syrup
              • • •
    ½ cup packed brown sugar
    ¼ cup butter or margarine, melted
    1 teaspoon ground cinnamon
    2 packages refrigerated buttermilk
        biscuits (20 biscuits)

Preheat oven to 375°. In saucepan combine cranberry-orange relish and light corn syrup; heat just to boiling. Spoon mixture into greased 6½-cup ring mold. Combine brown sugar, melted butter or margarine, and cinnamon. Spread one side of each biscuit with some of the brown sugar mixture. Stand biscuits on edge in ring mold. Bake at 375° till done, about 25 minutes. Allow to cool in pan 3 minutes. Invert onto serving plate. Makes 20 rolls.

Protein-Plus Muffins

Serve these delicious muffins with a soup or salad to increase the protein in the meal—

    1¼ cups soy flour
    ⅔ cup nonfat dry milk powder
    2 teaspoons baking powder
    ½ teaspoon salt
    ½ cup chopped pitted dates
    ¼ cup chopped walnuts
              • • •
    2 slightly beaten eggs
    1 teaspoon grated orange peel
    ¾ cup orange juice
    2 tablespoons honey
    2 tablespoons cooking oil

Preheat oven to 350°. In mixing bowl stir the soy flour, nonfat dry milk powder, baking powder, and salt together thoroughly. Stir in the chopped dates and chopped walnuts. Combine the beaten eggs, grated orange peel, orange juice, honey, and cooking oil. Stir the egg mixture into the dry ingredients just till moistened. Fill greased muffin cups ⅔ full. Bake at 350° till done, about 30 minutes. Makes 12 muffins.

Sour Cream-Chive French Loaves

    2 loaves unsliced French bread
    ¾ cup butter or margarine, softened
    ½ cup dairy sour cream
    2 tablespoons snipped chives
    ¼ teaspoon garlic powder

Preheat oven to 325°. Cut each loaf of bread lengthwise, then crosswise, *cutting to but not through* bottom crust. Mix remaining ingredients; spread on bread. Wrap in foil. Heat at 325° for 20 to 25 minutes. Serves 8.

Thyme-Buttered Crescents

    ½ cup butter or margarine, softened
    1 teaspoon lemon juice
    ½ teaspoon dried thyme, crushed
    1 package refrigerated crescent
        rolls (8 rolls)

Cream butter till fluffy. Stir in lemon juice and thyme. Keep herb butter at room temperature for 1 hour to mellow before using.
    Preheat oven. Unroll crescents; spread *2 teaspoons* herb butter on each crescent. Roll crescents up and bake according to package directions. Serve hot. Makes 8 rolls.

Raspberry Coffee Cake

    1 cup packed brown sugar
    ½ cup butter or margarine
    1 egg
    1 teaspoon vanilla
    2 cups all-purpose flour
    1 teaspoon baking soda
    ½ teaspoon baking powder
    1 8-ounce carton raspberry yogurt

Preheat oven to 350°. Cream sugar and butter; add egg and vanilla. Stir flour, soda, baking powder, and ¼ teaspoon salt together; add alternately with yogurt to creamed mixture. Mix well. Pour into greased 9-inch tube pan. Bake at 350° for 50 minutes. Remove from pan; sprinkle with powdered sugar, if desired. Serve warm or cool. Makes 1 coffee cake.

Fruit Compote Supreme

Keep this flavorful baked compote in mind for cold weather menus—

    1 16-ounce can peach slices
    1 cup dried apricots
    ½ cup packed brown sugar
    1 teaspoon grated orange peel
    ⅓ cup orange juice
    ½ teaspoon grated lemon peel
    2 tablespoons lemon juice
              • • •
    1 16-ounce can pitted dark sweet
      cherries, drained

Preheat oven to 350°. In 10x6x2-inch baking dish combine undrained peach slices, dried apricots, brown sugar, grated orange peel, orange juice, grated lemon peel, and lemon juice. Cover and bake compote at 350° for 45 minutes. Gently stir in the dark sweet cherries. Bake, covered, till cherries are heated through, about 15 minutes longer. Makes 6 to 8 servings.

Peanut Butter-Banana Crunch

A dessert the whole family will enjoy—

    4 cups sliced bananas (6 medium
      bananas)
    1 tablespoon lemon juice
    ½ teaspoon ground cinnamon
              • • •
    ½ cup all-purpose flour
    ½ cup packed brown sugar
    ⅓ cup chunk-style peanut butter
    3 tablespoons butter or margarine
      Whipped cream or whipped dessert
      topping (optional)

Preheat oven to 375°. Place sliced bananas in 8x1½-inch round baking dish. Add lemon juice and ground cinnamon, stirring lightly to coat fruit. In small mixing bowl combine flour and brown sugar; cut in chunk-style peanut butter and butter or margarine till mixture is crumbly. Sprinkle peanut butter mixture over bananas. Bake at 375° for 25 minutes. Serve warm; top with dollops of whipped cream or whipped dessert topping, if desired. Makes 6 servings.

Coconut-Peach Upside-Down Cake

A cake mix makes this extra easy—

    ½ cup packed brown sugar
    ¼ cup flaked coconut
    3 tablespoons butter or margarine,
      melted
    1 8-ounce can peach slices, drained
    1 package 1-layer-size yellow cake
      mix

Preheat oven to 350°. In 8x1½-inch round baking dish combine brown sugar, coconut, and melted butter or margarine. Pat evenly in bottom of dish. Arrange peach slices over coconut mixture. Mix cake according to package directions. Spread carefully over peaches. Bake at 350° till done, about 40 minutes. Cool 2 minutes in dish; invert on plate to serve. Makes 6 servings.

Sour Cream-Rhubarb Squares

    ½ cup granulated sugar
    ½ cup chopped walnuts
    1 tablespoon butter or margarine,
      melted
    1 teaspoon ground cinnamon
              • • •
    1½ cups packed brown sugar
    ½ cup shortening
    1 egg
    2 cups all-purpose flour
    1 teaspoon baking soda
    ½ teaspoon salt
    1 cup dairy sour cream
    1½ cups rhubarb cut in ½-inch
      pieces

Preheat oven to 350°. In small bowl mix granulated sugar, chopped walnuts, melted butter or margarine, and ground cinnamon till crumbly; set aside. Cream together brown sugar, shortening, and egg. Stir flour, baking soda, and salt together thoroughly; add to creamed mixture alternately with dairy sour cream. Stir in rhubarb pieces. Turn into greased and floured 13x 9x2-inch baking pan. Sprinkle with crumbly mixture. Bake at 350° for 45 to 50 minutes. Serve warm. Makes 9 to 12 servings.

Ginger-Pear Dessert

Serve warm with ice cream —

  4 medium pears
  ¼ cup orange juice
  1 cup finely crushed gingersnaps
  ¼ cup sugar
  ¼ cup chopped walnuts
  ¼ cup butter or margarine, melted
    Vanilla ice cream

Preheat oven to 350°. Peel pears; halve and core. Place pear halves, cut side up, in 10x6x2-inch baking dish. Drizzle with orange juice. Combine finely crushed gingersnaps, sugar, walnuts, and melted butter or margarine; sprinkle over pear halves. Bake at 350° till pears are tender, 20 to 25 minutes. Serve warm; top with scoops of vanilla ice cream. Makes 8 servings.

Cherry Crumbles

  1 21-ounce can cherry pie filling
  1 package 1-layer-size yellow cake
    mix
  ¼ cup butter or margarine, melted

Preheat oven to 375°. Spread pie filling in buttered 8x8x2-inch baking pan; sprinkle with the dry cake mix. Drizzle with melted butter or margarine (*do not stir*). Bake at 375° till top is golden, 35 to 40 minutes. Serve warm. Makes 8 servings.

Crab Apple-Peach Dumplings

Frozen patty shells speed up the preparation of this dessert (shown on page 75) —

  6 frozen patty shells, thawed
  6 canned peach halves
  6 spiced crab apples, cored and
    halved
  1 3-ounce package cream cheese, cut
    in 6 sticks
    Maple-flavored syrup *or* frozen
    whipped dessert topping

Preheat oven to 400°. Roll out each patty shell to a 6-inch circle. Top *each* with a peach half, 2 apple halves, and a stick of cream cheese. Moisten edges of dough; fold to center, forming a triangle. Seal. Bake at 400° till golden brown, 20 to 25 minutes. Serve topped with maple syrup or frozen whipped topping. Makes 6 servings.

Banana-Coconut Betty

  2 cups soft bread crumbs
    (2½ slices bread)
  6 tablespoons butter or margarine,
    melted
  ⅓ cup sugar
  2 teaspoons grated orange peel
  ½ teaspoon ground nutmeg
  ½ teaspoon ground cinnamon
  4 cups sliced banana (4 or 5)
  ¼ cup orange juice
  ¼ cup water
  ½ cup flaked coconut

Preheat oven to 375°. Toss crumbs with melted butter or margarine to coat. Line a 1½-quart casserole with *one-third* of the crumb mixture. Combine sugar, orange peel, nutmeg, and cinnamon. Cover crumbs with *half* the sliced banana and *half* the sugar mixture. Cover with another *one-third* of the crumbs, the remaining banana, and remaining sugar mixture. Combine orange juice and water; spoon over. Toss the remaining crumbs with flaked coconut; sprinkle over all. Bake, covered, at 375° for 30 to 35 minutes. Uncover; bake till golden, 5 to 10 minutes more. Makes 6 servings.

Special Helps

Does meal planning stump you? Are you concerned about good nutrition but not sure how to make meals nutritious? Do you have the supplies on hand to simplify cooking to fit your busy schedule?

On the following pages you'll find a wealth of important information that can help you. Use the meal planning ideas and the already-planned menus as guides for appetizing meals. Plan nutritious meals using the Basic 4 as explained on page 85. And stock your kitchen following the simple guidelines on page 92.

There are also hints to help you cook for one or two, a list of emergency substitutions, a glossary of basic cooking terms, and information on food storage.

Turn to this informative section frequently. It's here to help you make the most of all your resources.

Include this menu often in your meal plans. Your family will like the Ham-Potato Bake, Spicy Fruit Salad, *and* Mocha Toffee Parfaits. *(See the menu on page 88.)*

Meal Planning

Even if you work all day, you can prepare and serve delicious meals with a minimum of effort. But these appetizing meals don't just happen. They are planned.

As an after work cook, you know that the amount of time you have to prepare meals is one of the most important considerations in planning menus. However, your meals also must fit the budget and be nutritious, yet appeal to the family.

Set aside a time to plan the meals for the week. Write down the menus, making a detailed shopping list at the same time. This way you can save time shopping with a single trip to the store, and you can save preparation time because everything you need will be on hand.

Look through a variety of recipes and choose those that will fit your available time. After work meal preparation time is often short. Make the most of it by combining the three types of cooking pointed out in this book—make-ahead, jiffy, and easy. For instance, serve a make-ahead main dish with a jiffy salad and an easy dessert. By planning meal preparation, you won't be rushed. The menus on pages 86 to 89 are designed for after work preparation.

Scan the newspaper food ads for good buys. Take advantage of specials whenever you can. Use fresh fruits and vegetables in their seasons. These practices will contribute to economical menus.

Working people frequently miss breakfast and skimp on lunch. Such habits make it particularly hard to fulfill daily nutritional needs. To help make up for this, pay special attention to nutrition when planning meals (use the Basic 4, page 85, as a guide). Be sure that you get a good variety of dairy foods, vegetables and fruits, protein foods, and breads and cereals every day. Incorporate foods from the Basic 4 into your menus using the following steps:

1. Select a main dish that will provide each family member with at least one serving from the Meat Group.
2. Add a complementary food from the Bread-Cereal Group.

3. Include a hot or cold vegetable.
4. Choose a fruit or vegetable salad that complements the main dish.
5. Top off the meal with a dessert. Remember, fresh fruit makes a simple, yet nutritious dessert; and milk is the basis for puddings, custards, and malts.
6. Select a hot or cold beverage. This is an excellent place to fulfill the daily milk requirement.

But using the Basic 4 won't do any good if the food is tasteless or unattractive. Delicious meals depend on a successful blend of flavors and textures. The following tips will help plan the right food combinations:

• Serve a crisp food with a soft food.
• Accent a bland flavor with a zippy food.
• Season carefully to accent, not overwhelm the flavor. Usually, one highly seasoned food per meal is plenty.
• Plan a dessert that agrees with the meal— a light dessert with a hearty main dish, a rich dessert with a light meal.
• Accent hot foods with a cold food accompaniment. Temperature is important— serve hot foods hot and cold foods cold.
• Limit the number of mixtures served in a meal. For example, when serving a casserole, complement it with a lettuce wedge rather than with a tossed vegetable salad.
• A variety of shapes contributes to an appetizing meal. Fruits and vegetables, especially, can be served in many shapes— whole, sliced, wedged, cubed, and mashed.
• Add variety to meals with a new food, a new seasoning, or a new way of preparing an old favorite.
• Look also to eye appeal. If the entree has little color, serve a colorful vegetable or salad. Or accent it with a bright garnish— parsley, cherry tomatoes, or paprika.
• Make sure that the color of the plates and serving dishes doesn't overwhelm the food.
• A pleasing table setting greatly enhances the food's appearance. Take a few minutes before each meal to cover the table with place mats or a colorful tablecloth, set plates and silverware neatly, and perhaps even add a flower or other centerpiece.

Cooking for One or Two

Cooking in small quantities often poses a problem because most recipes serve four or more. This generally means that you cook a large meal and then eat leftovers for days or else you fix hamburgers and frozen dinners time after time. You can be more creative than this. Use the following suggestions and the recipes for two from this book (see list at beginning of index):

• If you have freezer space, freeze meats and leftover main dishes in meal-size portions. Leftovers will seem like new if you haven't had the dish for a while. Shape ground beef into patties before freezing. Wrap the beef patties individually in waxed paper or clear plastic wrap so you can use them one at a time.

• Buy frozen vegetables in plastic bags. Then, remove and cook just what's needed.

• Keep frozen fish on hand for quick meals. Cut the package of fish in half while frozen and return half to the freezer. Poach the fish in salted water and serve with hollandaise sauce made from a mix.

• Eggs and cheese are great for small-size entrées. For example, try omelets filled with leftover vegetables and bits of cooked meat, poached eggs topped with a cheese sauce, or grilled cheese sandwiches topped with a slice of tomato or onion.

• Add variety to meats with sauces and gravies made from mixes.

• Fill out meals with delicatessen foods.

• Create a main dish salad from lettuce, raw or cooked vegetables, cheese strips, croutons, strips of luncheon meat or leftover meat, and/or hard-cooked egg. Serve with your favorite salad dressing.

Recipe Terms to Know

Baste – To moisten foods during cooking with pan drippings or a flavorful sauce.
Beat – To make mixture smooth by briskly whipping or stirring with a spoon, rotary beater, or electric mixer.
Blend – To thoroughly mix two or more ingredients until smooth and uniform.
Chop – To cut in small pieces.
Cream – To beat with a spoon or electric mixer till smooth, light, and fluffy.
Cut in – To mix shortening with dry ingredients using pastry blender or knives.
Dice – To cut food into small cubes of uniform size and shape.
Flake – To break lightly into small pieces.
Fold – To add ingredients gently to a mixture. Using a spatula, cut down through mixture; go across bottom of bowl and up and over, close to surface. Turn bowl frequently for even distribution.
Grate – To rub on a grater that separates the food into very fine particles.
Knead – To work the dough with the heel of the hand with a pressing, folding motion.

Marinate – To allow a food to stand in a seasoned liquid.
Mince – To cut or finely chop food into very small pieces.
Partially set – To chill gelatin until the consistency of egg white.
Poach – To simmer in liquid, being careful that food holds its shape while cooking.
Roast – To cook uncovered without liquid added, usually in an oven.
Shred – To rub on a shredder to form long, narrow pieces.
Simmer – To cook in liquid over low heat so that bubbles form at a slow rate and burst before reaching the surface.
Soft peaks – To beat egg whites or whipping cream till peaks are formed when beaters are lifted, but tips curl over.
Stiff peaks – To beat egg whites till peaks stand up straight when beaters are lifted, but are still moist and glossy.
Whip – To beat rapidly to incorporate air and produce expansion, as in whipping cream or egg whites.

Think Good Nutrition

Does the phrase "eat a balanced diet" conjure up unpleasant memories of classroom lectures and scoldings from Mom and Dad? If so, it's time to revise your thinking and realize that practicing good nutrition is vital to your health. And that nutritious food is delicious.

It's easy to fall into poor nutritional habits. Perhaps you are too rushed to eat a good meal. Then, combine the four food groups into one dish such as a meat, tomato, and cheese sandwich or a macaroni, meat, tomato, and cheese skillet dish.

Or, maybe you don't like milk. If that's true, disguise milk by using it in cream sauces for meats or vegetables and in desserts such as custards and puddings.

Or, perhaps you live alone and it's too much bother to prepare a full meal, so you live on snacks. First, to take care of cooking in small quantities, look in the index on page 93 for a list of recipes for two servings given throughout the book. Then, use snacks as a nutritional supplement to meals. Eat fresh fruit instead of candy, a milk shake instead of pop, or a peanut butter sandwich instead of cookies.

Or, you might not be able to afford meat. Cut down meat costs by serving smaller portions (3 ounces lean cooked meat is an adequate portion); by making the meat go farther in casseroles, soups, stews, and main dish salads; and by planning some meals around protein foods other than meat.

As you can see, the reasons for poor nutrition could go on and on. However, by changing your ideas slightly, you can eliminate these stumbling blocks. In short, learn the Basic 4 (given at the right) and then *think good nutrition* at mealtime or whenever you eat.

Basic four ingenuity

← *For good health and good eating, plan daily meals that include the Dairy Group, the Meat Group, the Vegetable-Fruit Group, and the Bread-Cereal Group.*

Dairy Group: Milk is the primary source of calcium, which is needed for strong teeth and bones. It also provides protein, riboflavin, phosphorus, and vitamins A and D. Adults should drink *at least 2 cups daily;* teen-agers, 4 cups; children over nine, 3 cups; and children under nine, 2 to 3 cups. Cheese and ice cream may replace part of the daily requirement of milk. A 1-inch cube of Cheddar cheese=$\frac{2}{3}$ cup milk; $\frac{1}{2}$ cup cottage cheese=$\frac{1}{3}$ cup milk; 2 tablespoons cream cheese=1 tablespoon milk; and $\frac{1}{2}$ cup ice cream=$\frac{1}{4}$ cup milk.

Vegetable-Fruit Group: Include 4 or more *servings* from this group daily to provide vitamins C and A and other nutrients. Every day choose one top source of vitamin C (grapefruit, oranges, cantaloupe, broccoli, peppers, or strawberries) or two fair sources (cabbage, potatoes, spinach, tangerines, or tomatoes). Every other day serve a good source of vitamin A (apricots, broccoli, cantaloupe, carrots, dark green leaves, spinach, sweet potatoes, or winter squash).

Meat Group: These are the protein foods needed for growth and repair of body tissues. They also provide iron, thiamine, niacin, riboflavin, and other nutrients. You need *2 servings a day* from this group. One serving is 2 to 3 ounces of poultry, fish, or lean cooked meat; 2 eggs; 1 cup cooked dried beans, peas, or lentils; $\frac{1}{4}$ cup peanut butter; or 2 ounces Cheddar, American, or Swiss cheese.

Bread-Cereal Group: Whole grain, enriched, or restored breads and cereals are rich sources of thiamine, niacin, riboflavin, and other nutrients. Check package labels to be sure your choice has been enriched. Choose 4 *or more servings daily* from breads, cereals, cornmeal, crackers, flour, grits, macaroni, spaghetti, noodles, rice, quick breads, or other baked products. Count 1 slice of bread, 1 ounce of ready-to-eat cereal, or $\frac{1}{2}$ cup cooked cereal, rice, macaroni, or grits as one serving.

Menus

When preparing a meal, you may want to combine recipes for dishes that are prepared ahead, quickly, or leisurely. The following menus include recipes from all sections of this book. These various menus will enable you to fit your own after work time schedule.

Main Dish	Accompaniments	Salad	Dessert	Preparation Hints
Cauliflower-Tuna Ahoy (see page 8)	buttered French bread spiced peaches	lettuce wedge with Chili Mayonnaise (see page 52)	Mocha Toffee Parfaits (see page 56)	Prepare dressing and parfaits while main dish bakes. Serves 4.
Marinated Beef Tenderloin (see page 11)	Horseradish Bloody Mary (see page 26) Parker House rolls butter	Lemon-Blueberry Salad (see page 28)	Grasshopper Pie (see page 31)	Make-ahead menu for entertaining 6 guests. Serve the drink as an appetizer.
Apricot-Sauced Pork Chops (see page 10)	baked potatoes hard rolls butter	shredded cabbage with Herb Mayonnaise (see page 52)	Strawberry-Cheese Topping (see page 57) angel cake	Heat pork chops and bake the potatoes together in oven. Menu makes 6 servings.
Orange Chicken (see page 17)	Brown and Serve Potato Rolls (see page 29) buttered broccoli	radishes carrot sticks	brownies	Thaw only as many rolls as you need. Serves 3 or 4.
Oriental Skillet (see page 13)	chow mein noodles Thyme-Buttered Crescents (see page 77)	Spicy Fruit Salad (see page 28)	tapioca pudding	Make basic beef mixture for main dish ahead. Serves 4.
Sausage Lasagne (see page 19)	Toasted Bun Sticks (see page 54)	lettuce wedge Italian dressing	Speedy Strawberry Parfaits (see page 57)	Assemble lasagne casserole ahead, then bake with bun sticks. Makes 6 servings.
Sweet-Sour Chicken Mold (see page 22)	Horseradish Bloody Mary (see page 26) hot rolls		Blueberry-Orange Nut Bread (see page 30) whipped butter	Ideal luncheon menu. Make recipes ahead; serve drink as appetizer. Serves 8.
Dill-Sauced Salmon (see page 8)	Zucchini with Walnuts (see page 53) whole wheat rolls butter	orange and grapefruit sections Italian dressing	Strawberry-Peach Sundae (see page 56) vanilla ice cream	Extra special dinner for entertaining. Flame sundaes at the table. Serves 4.

Main Dish	Accompaniments	Salad	Dessert	Preparation Hints
Chicken Roll-Ups (see page 16)	Parslied Carrots (see page 76) hard rolls	molded fruit salad	lemon sherbet sugar cookies	Bake chicken and carrots together. Menu serves 4.
Barbecue-Sauced Kabobs (see page 37)	parslied rice cherry tomatoes celery	Orange Perfection Salad (see page 28)	angel cake	Prepare salad ahead. Serve kabobs with extra sauce. Serves 4.
Cheesy Tuna (see page 38)	baked patty shells	Tomato-Cucumber Marinade (see page 26)	Coconut-Peach Upside-Down Cake (see page 78)	An impressive, yet easy-to-prepare dinner menu for 6.
Ham Barbecue (see page 41)	hot cooked rice buttered green beans	fruit salad with Creamy Lime Dressing (see page 74)	Coffee-Banana Smoothee (see page 57)	The creamy-smooth dessert is made in a blender. Serves 2.
Saucy Poached Fish (see page 39)	hot cooked rice asparagus spears	orange slices	rum parfaits	Slice oranges while rest of meal cooks on range. Serves 4.
Beef-Tomato Skillet (see page 34)	hot cooked noodles	pear halves with Pink Fruit Dressing (see page 52)	chocolate pudding frozen whipped dessert topping	Cook main dish for 4 atop the range. Meal is ready to dish up in less than ½ hour.
Apricot-Glazed Ham (see page 41)	Potato-Vegetable Scallop (see page 76) hard rolls	lettuce wedge	Crab Apple-Peach Dumplings (see page 79)	Potatoes and dessert bake at the same temperature. Serves 6.
Oriental Chicken (see page 43)	chow mein noodles *or* hot cooked rice	tossed salad with Herb Mayonnaise (see page 52)	Chocolate Layer Pie (see page 31)	Fix pie ahead. Begin with a white dinner wine. Serves 4 to 6.
Sausage and Hashed Brown Omelet (see page 44)	rusks butter	sliced tomatoes	Polynesian Parfaits (see page 30)	An ideal supper menu. Makes 4 servings.
Creamed Turkey Especial (see page 43)	toasted English muffins	Curried Pear and Cheese Salad (see page 50)	Peanut Butter-Banana Crunch (see page 78)	Dessert bakes while you prepare turkey and salad. Serves 6.
Chicken-Wild Rice Skillet (see page 63)	hot rolls	cantaloupe wedge with green grapes	Pink Cream Dessert (see page 57)	Quick and easy menu for last-minute company. Serves 4.

Main Dish	Accompaniments	Salad	Dessert	Preparation Hints
Apple-Raisin Topped Ham (see page 64)	buttered corn Protein-Plus Muffins (see page 77)	Cottage Cheese-Cucumber Salad (see page 28)	pound cake	Ham and muffins bake together; make salad ahead. Serves 6.
Applesauce-Pork Loaf (see page 65)	baked potatoes	tossed green salad	ice cream cookies	Unusual applesauce-topped loaf will soon become a family favorite. Serves 4.
Oven Hamburgers (see page 67)	hot cooked noodles apple and orange slices	Lima Salad (see page 52)	Fruit Compote Supreme (see page 78)	Burgers and dessert bake together while you make the salad. Menu serves 6.
Swiss and Frank Pie (see page 69)	buttered carrots	sliced tomatoes and cucumbers with Herb Mayonnaise (see page 52)	Speedy Strawberry Parfaits (see page 57) ladyfingers	This main dish is nearly a complete meal in itself. Makes 6 servings.
Spaghetti Sauce (see page 69)	hot cooked spaghetti French bread with garlic butter buttered peas	orange slices and pineapple rings Italian dressing	Butter-Rum Sundae (see page 57)	Prepare spaghetti sauce first—then rest of meal. Menu serves 6.
Vegetable Chili (see page 73)	Thyme-Buttered Crescents (see page 77) carrot sticks cheese sticks	molded fruit salad	vanilla pudding	An extra-easy chili that uses frozen mixed vegetables. Makes 4 servings.
Ham-Potato Bake (see page 64) (shown on page 80)	relishes	Spicy Fruit Salad (see page 28)	Mocha Toffee Parfaits (see page 56)	Make salad ahead. While casserole bakes, make the parfaits. Serves 4 generously.
Oriental Stuffed Steaks (see page 68)	hard rolls broccoli with lemon butter	tossed salad with blue cheese dressing	Grasshopper Pie (see page 31)	An elegant menu for entertaining. Accompany with rosé. Menu makes 6 servings.
Polynesian Pork Steaks (see page 65)	mashed potatoes relishes	sliced tomatoes with French dressing	Crab Apple-Peach Dumplings (see page 79) maple syrup or frozen whipped topping	A good menu for a special family occasion for 6. Meat simmers while you fix the rest of the meal.

Main Dish	Accompaniments	Salad	Dessert	Preparation Hints
Stroganoff Steak Sandwiches (see page 21)	Festive Cheese Ball (see page 26)	Tomato-Cucumber Marinade (see page 26)	Chocolate Surprise Cake (see page 30)	Guests enjoy the appetizer while you take a little time to finish the sandwiches. Serves 6.
Ham Loaf Sandwiches (see page 20)	radishes celery	Cottage Potato Salad (see page 28)	assorted cookies	A tasty picnic menu. Pack the sandwiches and salad in an ice chest. Serves 6.
Potato-Topped Stew (see page 14)	Parsley-Onion Bread (see page 54)	sliced tomatoes	canned peaches	Make the stew ahead and freeze. Then, prepare the rest of the meal while stew bakes. Serves 4.
Meatball Hot Pot (see page 34)	Stir-Fried Green Beans (see page 53) hard rolls	Spicy Fruit Salad (see page 28)	angel cake	Guests participate in cooking the fondue-style main dish. Serves 4.
Broiled Meat Loaf (see page 36)	Sour Cream Potatoes (see page 54) carrots		Coffee-Banana Smoothee (see page 57)	A speedy meal for 2. Make the dessert in the blender.
Chicken Dinner Omelet (see page 44)	buttered carrots	lettuce wedge with Italian salad dressing	pound cake topped with strawberries	Delight a drop-in guest with this menu for 2 made with ingredients you can keep on hand.
Speedy Chicken Chasseur (see page 42)	buttered rice buttered peas	spiced peaches carrots	Polynesian Parfaits (see page 30)	The main dish is a fix-up for carry-out chicken. Serves 4.
Chicken Pilaf (see page 60)	cauliflower with Swiss-Dill Sauce (see page 53)	orange slices	butterscotch pudding	Fix the vegetable and salad quickly, then relax while the main dish bakes. Menu serves 2.
Hearty Chicken Soup (see page 73)	Protein-Plus Muffins (see page 77)	Cottage Cheese-Cucumber Salad (see page 28)	brownies	A perfect supper for a winter evening. Serves 6.

Food Storage Guide

Proper storage of food will save the food's good flavor and your money. So, promptly unpack groceries and store as directed:

Fresh Vegetables: Store white potatoes, sweet potatoes, onions, and winter squash unwashed in a cool, dry, dark place with good ventilation. Wash and thoroughly drain salad greens, celery, green onions, asparagus, and cabbage. Refrigerate separately in moisture-vaporproof bags. Remove tops of carrots, beets, and radishes; refrigerate separately in moisture-vaporproof bags. Husked sweet corn may be refrigerated in moisture-vaporproof bag for a short period of time. Leave peas in the pod and refrigerate.

Fresh Fruit: Remove injured fruit before storing. Refrigerate ripe tomatoes, apples, oranges, lemons, grapefruit, limes, kumquats, tangerines, peaches, apricots, cherries, grapes, pears, plums, and rhubarb in a loosely covered container or perforated moisture-vaporproof bag to reduce drying or wilting. Store bananas, melons, avocados, and pineapple at cool room temperature. Store berries in the refrigerator; wash before serving.

To ripen fruit, place in well-ventilated area at room temperature; avoid direct sunlight. Tomatoes, peaches, bananas, avocados, pears, and plums can be ripened this way. Refrigerate the ripened fruit, except bananas, till ready to use.

Dried Fruit, Nuts: Store dried fruit in tightly closed container at room temperature. Nuts will keep longer if refrigerated in tightly covered containers.

Canned Foods: Store in cool, dry place. After a canned food has been opened, cover the can and store in refrigerator.

Flour, Cereals: Store at room temperature in tight containers.

Dairy Products: Tightly cover cottage cheese, hard and soft cheeses, milk, and butter and store in the refrigerator. Place strong-flavored cheeses in a tightly covered jar and store in the refrigerator.

Eggs: Refrigerate in a covered container or in the original carton. You can keep egg yolks for 2 to 3 days by refrigerating in tightly covered container. Egg whites will keep for a week to 10 days if refrigerated in a tightly covered container.

Meat, Poultry, Fish: Fresh meat, paper-wrapped from the butcher, should be rewrapped loosely in waxed paper before refrigerating. You can refrigerate fresh meat prepackaged in moisture-vaporproof wrap as is. If meat is to be frozen, wrap in moisture-vaporproof freezer wrap to prevent drying out of the surface. (Prepackaged meat can be frozen for 1 to 2 weeks without rewrapping. For longer storage, open the package and rewrap in moisture-vaporproof freezer wrap.) Refrigerate cured meat and luncheon meat in original wrap. Most canned hams need refrigeration (see label instructions). Refrigerate fish in moisture-vaporproof bags or tightly covered containers. Cool and refrigerate cooked meat promptly; when chilled, cover the meat to prevent drying.

For maximum quality, store meat, poultry, or fish in the refrigerator or freezer only for the length of time recommended in the chart below.

Maximum Storage Time		
Meat or Poultry	Refrigerator (36°-40° F)	Freezer (0° F or lower)
Beef	2 to 4 days	6 to 12 months
Pork	2 to 4 days	3 to 6 months
Ground meats	1 to 2 days	3 months
Frankfurters	4 to 5 days	1 month
Bacon	5 to 7 days	1 month
Ham	1 week	2 months
Ham slices	3 to 4 days	2 months
Variety meats	1 to 2 days	3 months
Luncheon meats	1 week	don't freeze
Bulk pork sausage	1 week	2 months
Smoked sausage	3 to 7 days	don't freeze
Dry sausage	2 to 3 weeks	don't freeze
Cooked meats	4 to 5 days	2 to 3 months
Chicken	1 to 2 days	12 months
Turkey	1 to 2 days	6 months
Fish	1 to 2 days	6 to 9 months

Emergency Substitutions

For best recipe results, use the ingredients the recipe calls for. However, if you must substitute, consult the list in this chart.

In Place Of	Substitute
1 clove garlic	⅛ teaspoon garlic powder or instant minced garlic
1 small onion	1 teaspoon onion powder or 1 tablespoon instant minced onion, rehydrated
1 tablespoon fresh snipped herbs	1 teaspoon dried herbs
1 cup whipping cream, whipped	2 cups whipped dessert topping
1 cup cake flour	1 cup minus 2 tablespoons all-purpose flour
1 tablespoon cornstarch (for thickening)	2 tablespoons all-purpose flour or 4 teaspoons quick-cooking tapioca
1 cup sour milk or buttermilk	1 tablespoon lemon juice or vinegar plus whole milk to make 1 cup (let mixture stand 5 minutes before using)
1 1-ounce square unsweetened chocolate	3 tablespoons unsweetened cocoa powder plus 1 tablespoon butter or margarine
1 teaspoon dry mustard	1 tablespoon prepared mustard
1 cup tomato juice	½ cup tomato sauce plus ½ cup water
1 cup honey	1¼ cups sugar plus ¼ cup liquid
1 teaspoon baking powder	¼ teaspoon baking soda plus ½ cup buttermilk or sour milk (to replace ½ cup of liquid called for in recipe)
1 cup whole milk	½ cup evaporated milk plus ½ cup water or 1 cup reconstituted nonfat dry milk plus 2½ teaspoons butter or margarine
1 whole egg	2 egg yolks (for use in custards)
1 cup catsup or chili sauce	1 cup tomato sauce plus ½ cup sugar and 2 tablespoons vinegar (for use in cooked mixtures)
1 cake compressed yeast	1 package or 2 teaspoons active dry yeast

Stocking Your Kitchen

The after work cook (in fact, any cook) who has never stocked a kitchen before often has many problems. How many pots and pans should you buy? Which items from the variety of equipment do you really need? How do you know what is the best buy? What basic groceries must you have? The following guidelines will help you decide how to fill your kitchen with essentials:

• Purchase the best quality that you can afford. Remember, however, that high prices don't always mean good quality. Before buying a product, compare the material, design, special features, service contract, and warranty for different brands. Also read any available research studies.

• Pick out pieces that you can use for more than one job, such as freezer-to-oven-to-table baking dishes and casseroles and oven-going skillets.

• Every saucepan and skillet needs a securely fitting cover. Make sure that cover knobs and handles are made of a non-heat-conducting material.

• Avoid buying items with hard-to-clean cracks or unnecessary sharp edges.

• Make sure that each item is durable, stainproof, and rustproof.

• Look for seals of approval, standards, and testing. (Gas appliances should have the American Gas Association seal. Look for the Underwriters' Laboratory seal on all electrical equipment.)

• Read the warranty and make sure that servicing is readily available.

Basic kitchen equipment: The equipment needed for food preparation can be broken down into five groups—preparation, storage, cooking, cleaning, and serving. The variety of equipment available can be overwhelming, but remember that it isn't necessary to have everything. The following list is the equipment needed initially to supply a kitchen. Purchase other less essential equipment when necessary.

Preparation: Can opener, carving knife, slicer, grater or shredder, vegetable peeler, potato masher, kitchen shears, vegetable brush, pair of tongs, strainers, two paring knives, colander, serrated knife, electric mixer, nested set of dry measuring cups, wooden spoons, flour sifter, measuring spoons, rotary beater, set of mixing bowls, bottle opener, liquid measuring cup, rubber spatulas, rolling pin with cover, and pastry cloth.

Storage: Refrigerator/freezer, assorted refrigerator-freezer dishes, cupboards, foil, clear plastic wrap, bread box, canisters, and waxed paper.

Cooking: Covered skillets (10- and 7- to 8-inch), covered saucepans (1-, 2-, and 4- to 6-quart), range with oven, square baking pans, wire cooling rack, coffee maker, pancake turner, long-handled fork, toaster, long-handled spoon, oblong baking pan (13x9x2), round baking pans, loaf baking dish (8½x4½x2½), roasting pan with rack, muffin pan, custard cups, casserole with cover, cookie sheets, potholders, hot pads, and pie plates.

Cleaning: Sink, dishpan, dishcloth and towels, wastebasket, draining rack and mat, garbage pail, and wastepaper basket.

Serving: Serving bowls, dinner and salad plates, platter, sauce dishes, cups, saucers, glasses, table linen, and silverware.

Basic groceries: Most foods you buy are a matter of preference, but there are some things you can't cook without. Buy these things in quantities that you can use up within a reasonable amount of time. When buying perishable foods, choose the form— fresh, canned, dried, or frozen—that best fits your needs and storage facilities. When you start to run low on an item, jot it down for your next shopping trip.

Always keep these foods on hand: Sugar, all-purpose flour, salt, pepper, baking powder, baking soda, coffee and/or tea, shortening, salad oil, butter and/or margarine, your favorite herbs and spices, vanilla, mayonnaise and/or salad dressing, prepared mustard, Worcestershire sauce, catsup, bread, eggs, meat, salad greens, vegetables, fruits, juices, and milk.

INDEX

D-I